The MORAL DIMENSIONS *of* MARRIAGE *and* FAMILY THERAPY

August G. Lageman

Ron
with appreciation
for our good
times at F.X.
Monmouth
August

UNIVERSITY
PRESS OF
AMERICA

Lanham • New York • London

Copyright © 1993 by
University Press of America®, Inc.
4720 Boston Way
Lanham, Maryland 20706

3 Henrietta Street
London WC2E 8LU England

Library of Congress Cataloging-in-Publication Data

Lageman, August G.
The moral dimensions of marriage and family therapy / by August G.
Lageman.
p.   cm.
Includes bibliographical references and index.
1. Marital psychotherapy.   2. Family psychotherapy.   3. Marriage—
Moral and ethical aspects.   I. Title.
RC488.5.L3485   1993   174'.2—dc20   92–33573 CIP

ISBN 0–8191–8965–0 (cloth : alk. paper)
ISBN 0–8191–8966–9 (pbk. : alk. paper)

The paper used in this publication meets the minimum requirements of
American National Standard for Information Sciences—Permanence
of Paper for Printed Library Materials, ANSI Z39.48–1984.

Contents

Preface

This book arises from two parts of my professional experience—the first as a clinician working in the field of marriage and family therapy and the second as an associate faculty member of The College of Notre Dame in Baltimore, Maryland, teaching in the field of moral philosophy. As I taught courses in ethics, I frequently took examples from my clinical work. This began an interactive process which has continued for the last six years.

In the clinical world there are often attempts made to stay value neutral—an effort arising, I believe, from a widespread fear of being seen as moralistic. Therapy is nonetheless a value laden activity, with the value systems of therapist and client continually in the process of interacting. In the early 1960s Perry London, in his book *Modes and Morals of Psychotherapy,* reflected on the moral dimensions of psychotherapy.[1] London points out that there are significant differences depending on whether the therapist works with emotions, thoughts and insights, or focuses on relationships and behaviors. In the first instance emotions and thoughts have traditionally been regarded as "premoral goods," essentially outside the realm of morality. Thoughts and feelings, the saying goes, are neither right or wrong. Yet it is also true that actions spring from thoughts and emotions. Accordingly, sharp distinctions between the moral relevance of emotions and thoughts on the one hand, and behaviors on the other, is both artificial, and in some cases, dangerous.

For example, in my experience as a marital therapist, couples are interacting on the various levels of thoughts, feelings, and behaviors in an ongoing and fluid

---

[1]London, Perry. *The Modes and Morals of Psychotherapy.* 2nd ed., New York: McGraw-Hill, 1986.

interactive process. When I stop the action by focusing on one of these dimensions, I am attempting to help by clarifying what is going on. Another example is a client with suicidal ideations. In some cases therapists have kept the focus on the realm of thoughts and feelings, assuming that correcting irrational thoughts and venting painful emotions are the essential ingredients of the healing process. By refusing to focus on behaviors and relationships the therapist is ruling out a significant dimension of human life and at the same time denying that a specific behavior (the act of suicide) may occur. The fatal assumption here is that because the therapist draws a clear distinction so does the client.

London points out that while psychotherapy grew up in a medical context, a stronger case can be made for viewing therapy in a moral context. I agree with London's thesis and this book is an examination of how viewing marriage and family therapy in a moral context can expand our abilities to understand and help our clients. Thomas Kuhn's concept of paradigms (a series of assumptions which make up a framework) has had considerable influence in the philosophy of science.[2] My thesis is that therapy is a value laden activity that needs to be understood in various contexts, but that a moral paradigm is fundamental to the practitioners understanding the nature of marriage and family therapy.

Values are recognized as the most difficult aspect of a person's belief system to change. Indeed, this gives rise to the first question: Who gives the right to a therapist to attempt to change a client's value system? Marriage and family therapy literature consistently talks about changing behaviors. We are, in effect, involved in the process of influencing people and their relationships. If we are to avoid maternalistic and

---

[2]Kuhn, Thomas S. *The Structure of Scientific Revolutions*. 2nd ed., Chicago: University of Chicago Press, 1970.

paternalistic stances, we need to relate in ways that respect client value systems. Yet there are clear limits to this respect: when, for example, client value systems generate cruel and violent treatment of others.

I will argue that marriage and family therapists *need to respect and work within client value systems and that attempts to change these value systems must normally be preceded by the clients' requests.* The following case is an example of a value dilemma that clinicians frequently face.

Case

A forty-two year old man seeks therapy for himself. His presenting problem is chronic dissatisfaction with his twenty year marriage. The couple has three children, ages seventeen, thirteen, and nine. The man wrestles with a dilemma: should he stay in the marriage or should he seek a divorce? The therapist also has a dilemma: work with the man alone or push to see the couple (or even the entire family). To divorce would be to better the client emotionally (and relationally in the long run). Does he put his well-being above that of the rest of his family? Or does he try to adapt further to a lifeless marriage, sacrificing part of himself and partially benefiting his children? What is the "right" thing to do?

The therapist has a responsibility to help such a client understand his dilemma in the context of the client's own values and morals. There are two ways to proceed. The first is to help the client change his values, but only if the client wants to change some of his values. The other alternative is to help the client find a solution within his existing value system. I maintain that the choice of these alternatives should depend primarily on what the client is requesting, not on the solution that the therapist prefers or thinks is best; and I will show that this position is both ethically and clinically sound.

My personal goals for this book are fourfold.

My first goal is to sharpen the reader's ability to recognize and understand moral issues. This book is an interactive process between what goes on in family therapy and relevant moral theory. Practitioners sometimes miss significant moral issues because they define the issues in clinical terms and concepts. Implied and even hidden moral issues need to be brought to the surface.

The second goal is to involve the right brain in the moral process and to stimulate the moral imaginations of my readers. Truth, as Nietzsche pointed out, is "a mobile army of metaphors," by which he is suggesting that truth is multiple and fluid.[3] This goal also involves the use of literature and metaphors. For example, Jane Austin, in her final book *Persuasion*, develops a feminine notion of constancy in relationships which plays a key role in the discovery of the self.[4] Constancy in relating to our clients is a prime ingredient in the therapeutic process.

A third goal is to elicit a sense of moral obligation and personal responsibility. This involves giving readers clear pictures and visions of themselves as moral agents. I am attempting to counteract the "minimalist attitude" found in our culture which in the name of tolerance makes a virtue out of demanding as little as possible both from ourself and others.

My last goal is paradoxical. It is to create both a tolerance of and resistance to ambiguity. Contemporary professional life is filled with dilemmas which do not allow a simple, neat answer. It is important to both recognize and develop a tolerance for this ambiguity. At the same time I believe that there are situations we try to avoid by describing the dilemma and then walking away. In many situations we need to work through the ambiguity and reach a clear moral conclusion. I will try to show there is no

---

[3]Quoted in Rorty, Richard. *Contingency, Irony, and Solidarity*. New York: Cambridge University, 1989, 17.

[4]Austin, Jane. *Persuasion*. New York: Bantam, 1974. See also John Beede's chapter "Integrity and Gender" in *Integrity in Depth*. College Station Texas: Texas A & M University Press, 1992, pp. 70–98.

preset formula (like a code of ethics) that tells us when to tolerate and when to resist ambiguity.

Because this book pursues these goals and integrates marriage and family therapy at a deeper level, it is intended to be used by the practitioner and as a college text on both undergraduate and graduate (professional school) levels. It is an integration of moral philosophy with the field of marriage and family therapy. Thus both the practitioner and the student preparing for practice can benefit from this book.

I am grateful to my clients and colleagues at the Pastoral Counseling Services of Maryland for providing an affirming context in which to work and grow and to my students and colleagues at The College of Notre Dame in Baltimore, Maryland who have provided a stimulating and challenging context for my teaching.

Foreword

These are exceedingly trying times to be a practitioner in the helping professions, particularly the psychotherapeutic and counseling fields. From within these professions, there is a kind of internecine warfare going on among psychiatrists, psychoanalysts, clinical psychologists, psychiatric social workers, and counselors of various schools and orientations. Each is attempting to achieve its fair share of professional status and public confidence, and each is attempting to expand or to maintain its niche in a mental health care system riddled with economic rationing and questionable priorities. Who are the most profitable patients and clients? Who is most in need? Who can be helped, and by what type of therapy?

From outside the helping professions, persistent doubts and worries continue to be expressed as well. Government policy makers and private insurance companies are leery of the costs that these professional services entail, and are suspicious of the lasting effectiveness of "soft" and holistic therapies that manifestly depart from the medical model. Social critics and intellectuals, such as Philip Reiff, Alasdair MacIntyre, Robert Bellah, Christopher Lasch, and the late Michael Foucault, have raised searching—and often persuasive—questions about the larger social and cultural implications of what Reiff originally called "the triumph of the therapeutic."

Many of these questions have to do with power—the power the helping professions exercise over their clients and over the social programs of the bureaucratic welfare state; and the conceptual power that value-laden notions, such as health, dysfunction, normalcy, adjustment, and even happiness, have in our cultural images and aspirations. Should professionals trained in a particular therapeutic paradigm be the de facto arbiters of the meaning of these fundamental terms? It is perhaps not surprising that philosophers and theologians are often the ones asking these awkward questions, for it is precisely their role as the cultural definers of these terms that the helping professions have usurped.

No less disturbing, perhaps, is the suspicion that the helping professions have contributed—sometimes unwittingly, sometimes deliberately—to an erosion of a sense of moral right and wrong. The very notions of "therapy," "dysfunctional" families, and the like are more apt to suggest problems of communication than of character. Blaming the victim is one of the cardinal mistakes in the therapeutic worldview: counselors advise, healers heal; they do not condemn and they do not judge.

And yet, despite these quarrelsome times in which the helping professions find themselves, people continue to seek help in increasing numbers. Our society evidently needs the services, skills, and expertise of the helping professions, more so now than ever before. The pain and the individual and social troubles are all around us, cutting across all lines of class, color, and ethnicity. Drug and alcohol abuse, divorce, domestic violence, sexual harassment, homelessness, depression, suicide—the signs of our profound anguish and suffering in contemporary society are intolerable. They cannot—they must not—be ignored or papered over by nostalgia for simpler times or ideological slogans about traditional or family values. For all the questioning and the uncertainty, this is precisely the time when we need to attract the best and the brightest, the most socially conscientious and the most caring, into the helping professions. This is the time, also, when the ethical nature and commitment of professionalism in all the helping professions most urgently needs to be addressed and transmitted to the younger generation of practitioners.

Dr. August Lageman has done us a timely service in this book. Marriage and family therapy is a growing field, which, in effect, is only now undergoing the difficult process of professionalization. Drawing from the scholarly resources of professional ethics in many kindred fields, and with an impressive command of the philosophical theories undergirding standards of professional ethics, Dr. Lageman achieves two very important goals in *The Moral Dimensions of Marriage and Family Therapy*.

First, he provides a unique and valuable text for students in the field. It provides an essential bridge between ethical theory and marriage and family counseling practice. It gives students the tools they need to think clearly about the difficult moral choices and decisions they will face in everyday practice.

Dr. Lageman's second achievement is equally significant, and gives the book an importance in the field of marriage and family therapy that goes beyond its interest as an ethics text for students. It shows vividly how family therapy can and should deal with the persistent questions of power and responsibility mentioned above. The power of therapists and the vulnerability of clients are put in their proper perspective. The power of the therapist is sufficient to create the need for moral boundaries, duties, and virtues, and these are described in concrete detail. But Dr. Lageman recognizes that professional ethics in marriage and family therapy cannot be solely individualistic and client-centered in orientation, for it is not so much isolated individuals as relationships that the therapist must strengthen and restore. For me, some of his most challenging and pointed arguments come out of the recognition that to heal relationships sometimes means to challenge the moral character of the individuals in those relationships. Healing also means—pace the social critics of the therapeutic ethos, challenging the broader social context within which those relationships are lived out in such compromised and troubled ways.

This is not prejudiced moralizing, but it is not a bland, blameless relativism either. In Dr. Lageman's eloquent case for ethical professionalism, one hears the experienced counselor and healer who knows that real life is a place where relationships are messy and complex, and where no simple codes or answers will provide a panacea. But behind this voice of worldly experience, one hears echoes of the prophet, too. The prophet who won't let us get away with our self-serving excuses or with evasions of responsibility for our own lives and commitments to others. This is a voice that will lead the helping professions out of their current wilderness and toward a richer vision of human flourishing and the common good.

Bruce Jennings
Executive Director, The Hastings Center

Chapter 1

The Wider Contexts: Social Structures and Professional

Ideologies

PREJUDICE

The practice of marriage and family therapy takes place in a social order replete with both prejudice and violence. Violence is usually thought of as overt physical harm to another. Prejudice is a form of violence which can be defined as those attitudes and forms of speech which demean people and regard them as less than fully human. Prejudice involves stereotypical thought patterns and attitudes which label people. Often prejudice is the projection onto other groups negative and undesirable characteristics. African-Americans, women, Jews, and Arabs are but a few of the groups that have been the targets of prejudice.

I maintain that marriage and family therapists have a responsibility to confront the various forms of prejudice in the treatment process. For example, clients refer to their neighbors in terms of offensive ethnic and racial slurs. Some therapists view this from a psychodynamic perspective as the discharge of hostile feelings. I believe we have a responsibility to find ways of helping clients examine these attitudes and seeing how such attitudes are destructive of themselves and others. Robert Jay Lifton has examined the ways in which we define the other as nonhuman. Lifton traces this process, which has in our century culminated in the Holocaust, in his book *The Nazi Doctors: Medical Killing and the Psychology of Genocide.*[1] Peter

---

[1]Lifton, Robert Jay. *The Nazi Doctors: Medical Killing and the Psychology of Genocide.* New York: Basic Books, 1986.

Haas points out that the process began when Jews were first seen as outsiders.[2] When other groups of people are seen as "different from," there is the danger that "different from" becomes "less than," and the formation of prejudicial attitudes begins. Thomas Ogletree rightly suggests that "hospitality to the stranger" is a key metaphor for the moral life. Moral reflections must begin in an inclusive rather than an exclusive direction. Ogletree points out that:

> Hospitality has relevance to the human assault on oppressive social structures, though its bearing on relations between oppressor and oppressed, or even between beneficiaries and victims of social oppression, is ambiguous. To be oppressed is to be virtually without a home. It is not only to be structurally vulnerable to those who wield power; it is also to be forced to work out of a sense of self within a context determined by the definitions, priorities, and interests of the oppressor.[3]

Beginning to reflect on social prejudice and its destructive effects gives us reason to challenge the idea that therapy is a value neutral enterprise. Our human responsibility, whether as therapists or private citizens, includes confronting dehumanizing values and becoming a part of the process which changes them.

It is important to recognize that the effects of prejudice rest not only with the victims, but with its perpetrators as well. Robert Bly has explored how male chauvinist attitudes and beliefs have both emotionally and relationally impoverished men.[4] Part of the patriarchal picture views men as superior in the ways of the

---

[2]Haas, Peter J. *Morality After Auschwitz: The Radical Challenge of the Nazi Ethic.* Philadelphia: Fortress Press, 1988.

[3]Ogletree, Thomas. W. *Hospitality to the Stranger: Dimensions of Moral Understanding.* Philadelphia: Fortress Press, 1985, 4–5.

[4]Bly, Robert. *Men and the Wound—The Naive Male.* St. Paul: Ally Press, 1988.

world, but at the same time emotionally inadequate in terms of relationships. Chauvinistic attitudes limit and impoverish relationships within the family.

Case

A blue collar family comes in for family therapy. The couple has two children, a boy twelve and a girl ten. The boy is doing well in school while his sister is having difficulty academically and socially. In the initial sessions it is clear that the father puts down his daughter and attacks her self-esteem. The father is often critical of his son but has become "buddies" with him, and they share several hobbies.

The presenting problem is the daughter's difficulties academically and socially. The basic task is to help the father recognize and eliminate his put-downs of his daughter. The father needs to see how the same way of relating is hurting his son. The key issue is helping the family in general and the father in particular understand how male chauvinist attitudes and the collusion with these values are a major source of the problem that has brought them in for therapy. The therapist needs to help the father understand how his attitudes and ways of relating to his children contribute to their low self-esteem. At the same time we recognize that the father's put-downs are both ways of masking and externalizing his own low self-esteem. The father sees his daughter in terms of a stereotype that girls are not supposed to do well academically. This limits her, and at the same time by focusing on the daughter, the father's superior posture helps him to avoid examining the roots of his own low self-esteem.

Therapists who maintain a value neutral position would attempt to resolve the issue without explicit attention to the prejudice involved and its social dimensions, thus splitting life into private and social realms. This splitting, or "bifurcation," is a fundamental problem in both our profession and in our society. Family therapists, along with other mental health professionals, have a particular responsibility for healing the bifurcation between public and private life, because we know intimately how they interpenetrate one another from hearing our clients' stories. Research is being conducted on how the private and political realms are interwoven and interconnected. Susan Griffin, in *A Chorus of Stones: The Private Life of War*, demonstrates how child rearing practices get translated into history and then back again.[5]

Griffin describes the violence of Heinrich Himmler's childhood and shows how this formed his personality and in part enabled his central role in the atrocities of the Nazi movement. There are other examples, both positive and negative, of this type of personality analysis which Griffin describes. The violence and abandonment of Saddam Hussein's childhood helps us to understand him and his style of leadership. In contrast, the positive influences of Michael Gorbachev's mother played a key role in shaping the Soviet leader's values and personality. Alice Miller, in *For Your Own Good: Hidden Cruelty in Child Rearing and the Roots of Violence,* examines the interactive process between violence in child rearing practices and the epidemic of violence in our world.[6]

The Holocaust is the legacy of the twentieth century and the horrible witness to what can happen when the process of prejudice goes unchecked. The process begins in part when people isolate themselves from their social order and their history. It is our responsibility as clinicians to do what we can to overcome the

---

[5]Griffin, Susan. From the manuscript of the as yet unpublished *A Chorus of Stones: The Private Life of War.*

[6]Miller, Alice. *For Your Own Good: Hidden Cruelty in Child Rearing and the Roots of Violence.* Translated by Hildegaard and Hunter Hannum. New York: Farrar, Straus, and Geroux, 1983.

bifurcation of life into unrelated private and public realms which provide the soil from which prejudice grows.

THE CRISIS IN PROFESSIONALISM

The problems in our social order are reflected in a growing loss of confidence in our institutions and our professions. Another more immediate context of our work as family therapists is the crisis within professional life in our society. In the last decade the erosion of trust in professionals has reached alarming proportions. Robert Kanigel describes the symptoms as, "...red tape, malpractice suits, recredentializing, cost control, and general distrust."[7] For Kanigel, the most common and distressing symptom is burnout, which is found within each of the professions. Another pressing symptom is the increasing number of lawsuits. Increasingly, professional organizations are trying to police their own members, but only with partial success.

There are at least four major sources of this crisis. The first source is the various ideologies that support the idea of professions. John Kultgen argues that there are four premises on which professions base their position and prestige: independence, altruism, peer review, and wisdom.[8] The medical profession, for example, as a whole has not led the society toward a just distribution of medical services. With the persistent tendency of all professions to see themselves in

---

[7]Kanigel, Robert. "The Endangered Professional." *Johns Hopkins Magazine,* 1988, 1.

[8]Kultgen, John. "The Ideological Use of Professional Codes." *Business and Professional Ethics Journal* 1 (Spring 1982): 53–69.

idealistic terms, the newly emerging profession of marriage and family therapy needs to engage in critical reflection on its ideological basis. I will begin this reflection in the second part of this chapter.

A second source of the crisis in professional life is linguistic in nature. In teaching college courses in professional ethics, I became aware that the word "professional" was being used so vaguely and broadly as to become a synonym for "good." The word "professional" then applies to every type of activity when it is "well done." A central issue emerges: "What constitutes a profession?" Originally in Western society there were only three professions, medicine, law, and theology. Largely because these professionals have been well paid and respected, the practitioners of countless occupations have aspired to professional status. Thus it appears that the professionalization of Western society is a never-ending process. In an attempt to focus this issue, I propose that we establish at least a minimal definition of what constitutes a profession—a theoretical body of knowledge, specialized training, and a commitment to serve people. Otherwise, we have more than a linguistic problem, because we are caught in a never-ending process of professionalization that will ultimately render the idea of a "profession" meaningless.

The third source of the crisis is that professions have tended to operate out of hierarchical paradigms. A hierarchical paradigm views the professional in a supervisor position relative to the client. The professional possesses knowledge-based power over the client. Robert Veatch describes four possible models for the physician-patient relationship.[9] In the engineering model the physician is the expert who presents medical information. In this model the physician is the scientific expert using knowledge and skill to heal the patient. The second model is the priestly, in which the physician gives paternalistic advice. In the priestly view the physician knows best and is seen as the dispenser of wisdom. Clearly both the engineering and priestly models involve a hierarchical position from which the client is helped. For Veatch, there are two additional possibilities. The collegial model suggests that the client and professional function as partners, i.e., as colleagues. Veatch rejects this approach because of the gap in knowledge between the client and professional. Instead, Veatch opts for a contractual model which keeps the roles separate and distinct while allowing the client and the professional to remain on equal footing because their relationship is based upon a mutually agreed upon contract for professional services.

Family therapists have operated out of each of these models. In the engineering model the therapist knows expert techniques and uses them to help families solve problems. Similarly, in the priestly model, the therapist is the dispenser of wisdom to families. In terms of family therapy, the collegial model tends to blur the distinct roles of therapist and client. The contractual model is the most appropriate one for family therapists. It keeps the roles distinct yet allows for equality on a contractual level.

The emergence of professions in general and family therapy in particular from the hierarchical models is a crucial development. The power imbalance inherent

---

[9]Veatch, Robert. *Models for Ethical Medicine in A Revolutionary Age.* Briarcliff Manor NY: Hastings Center, 1972.

within the hierarchical models in part accounts for the increasing number of complaints from clients involving abuse of power and unjust treatment. Family therapists are working in the midst of a significant shift from hierarchical models to more collaborative models of viewing the therapeutic process.

The fourth source of our present crisis is institutional in nature. Professions themselves now serve as institutions:

> We have, it seems, a built in negativity toward institutions. A major reason why organizations and institutions are often viewed as either morally neutral or morally negative is that, as they grow larger and become more systematic about the pursuit of their ends, they inevitably become more bureaucratic. Bureaucracies tend to be hierarchical, specialized, and impersonal. Roles narrow, paperwork proliferates, and layers pile up in the name of efficiency. The personal touch may get lost in the process.[10]

Many family therapists work in a variety of social service institutions. Our clients not only share the growing mistrust of professionals but also the prevailing negative view of institutions. Many of our clients work in large institutions and a part of the reason they come to therapy is to recover the personal dimension of existence. Family therapists either practice privately (without a direct institutional context) or long to be in private practice.

Yet there is an additional dimension in that as Eric Mount points out that our professions themselves now function as our institutional habitats.[11] Thus, the American Association of Marriage and Family Therapists (AAMFT) is a particular institution which functions as our institutional habitat. American professionals of

---

[10] Mount, Eric. *Professional Ethics in Context.* Louisville: Westminster/John Knox Press, 1990, 34.

[11] *ibid.,* 39.

every sort, rightly or not, tend to feel more strongly about their loyalties to their clients than to their professions. Eric Mount gives a clear political example of this:

> As David Price, now a member of the U. S. House of Representatives from North Carolina, and Richard Flenno have alleged, legislators tend to accentuate their personal ties with the electorate and downplay their responsibility for making the legislature work well as an institution.[12]

It is clear that as family therapists we need to examine the institutional contexts where we practice as well as our professional organizations which function as institutional habitats influencing our attitudes, providing ideological contexts that shape how we view ourselves and our work as family therapists.

SOCIAL STRUCTURES

Both as professionals and as private citizens we live and work within the structures that make up our society. The various professions have not for the most part attempted to alter unjust social and economic systems. Magali Larson, in *The Rise of Professionalism*, points out that professional groups have attempted to win a place in the hierarchy of occupations and have not tried to alter economic systems.[13] Thus, the power struggle does not occur on a societal level but rather within class lines.

In *The Credentialed Society*, a study of the role of education in social stratification, Randall Collins points out that our society has moved from a society of ascription to one of achievement.[14] Where power and privilege were once

---

[12]*ibid.*, 38.

[13]Larson, Magali Sarfatti. *The Rise of Professionalism*. Berkeley: University of California Press, 1977.

[14]Collins, Randall. *The Credentialed Society*. New York: Academic Press, 1979.

assigned according to family or political connections, society has shifted to assigning power and prestige to the professional. In this shift the university is pivotal in that it identifies and trains professionals.

Part of the reality of our social order is that professional services are not distributed widely enough to reach all those who need them.[15] With some exceptions, the health-related professions have for the most part been a middle and upper class phenomenon.

John Kultgen, in *Ethics and Professionalism,* argues for the establishment of a professional charter which would clearly define the professions' responsibility to society:

> The primary function of a charter would be to define responsibilities. In an organic society, lawyers would be assigned special, though not exclusive, responsibility for the preservation and improvement of the legal system; medical professionals, for the system of health care; engineers, for the protection of the environment and conservation of resources, etc. Existing professions give mere lip service to these responsibilities would define exactly who is responsible, for what groups of people or aspects of peoples' welfare and to whom.[16]

Robert Veatch, working primarily in the field of bioethics, points out that people, not just health care professionals, make medical decisions. Veatch argues that: "...there is no reason why other health professionals or laypersons should accept these principles [AMA Code of Ethics], yet each of these groups has an

---

[15]May, William. "The Beleaguered Rulers: The Public Obligations of the Professionals." *Kennedy Institute of Ethics Journal* 2 (1992): 25–41.

[16]Kultgen, John. *Ethics and Professionalism.* Philadelphia: University of Pennsylvania Press, 1988, 163.

important role in medical decisions."[17] From Veatch's point of view all elements of society should have a say in the formulation of ethics.

Veatch maintains that there are three contracts involved in doing medical ethics.[18] The first contract is a basic social contract in which the members of society agree on the principles of social interaction. The next contract is a covenant between society and the health-related professions. The third contract is between individual physicians and patients. The provisions of the second contract are derived from the first; and contracts on the third level are derived from the second. Veatch's triple contract provides family therapists with a framework that considers the social order and raises the issue of the professions' contract (or charter) with society.

As we have seen, Veatch opposes the idea that the profession by itself sets the moral parameters for its work. Veatch points out the absence of any epistemological basis for a claim of greater moral insight by professionals.[19]

Accepting the first two dimensions of the social contract opens professional ethics to the issues of justice and liberation—which are not often at the center of reflection in professional ethics. Family therapists have a responsibility to work to change social and political forces which have, for example, created ghettos in our major cities. People who live in our ghettos find the idea of being a "client" foreign to them. People coming from these environments are often depressed, although it may be more accurate to see them as oppressed. To diagnose a person as oppressed is to open the door to dealing with the social forces that have produced this

---

[17]Veatch, Robert. *A Theory of Medical Ethics*. New York: Basic Books, 1981, 6, 16–17, 132.

[18]*ibid.*, 110–126.

[19]*ibid.*, 98–99.

oppression. Our task then becomes one of social change and liberation. Karen

Lebacqz, in *Professional Ethics: Power and Paradox*, points out that,

> To put justice and liberation at the heart of professional ethics is quite different from the usual view. In the usual view, the dominant norm for professional is beneficence—doing good for the client. Most ethical dilemmas are seen as a conflict between beneficence and some other norm, such as truth telling or keeping confidence.[20]

Lebacqz goes on to maintain that being a professional involves working for a

balance of power that can be described as justice.

PROFESSIONAL IDEOLOGIES

Sociologists have been examining the role of professions in Western society.

John Kultgen sees two fundamentally different models of the role of professions in

society.[21] The functionalist model views the professions as a positive force in social

development standing against the excesses of both laissez-faire individualism and

state collectivism. Historically, this view goes back to the French sociologist Emile

Durkheim. Durkheim thought that the professions would become communities that

would cultivate order, discipline, and duty at a time when moral institutions were

being dissolved by the fragmentation of labor.[22]

The other model is described by Kultgen as the conflict model. Theorists

supporting this view see professionalism as a negative force. Conflict theorists

expect to find dysfunction not only in human beings but also in social institutions.

---

[20]Lebacqz, Karen. *Professional Ethics: Power and Paradox*. Nashville: Abingdon Press, 1985, 129.

[21]Kultgen, John. *Ethics and Professionalism*. Philadelphia: University of Pennsylvania Press, 1988, 62–64.

[22]*ibid.*, 62.

Both Larson, in *The Rise of Professionalism,* and Collins, in *The Credentialed Society,* are proponents of this view.

The conflict model is not widely known in the profession of family therapy; and where it is known it is not liked because of its negative view of the profession. The functionalist model, however, is part of contemporary professional ideology because it sees the profession in beneficent terms. We like to see ourselves as oriented to public service. Both the idealism of the functional model, as well as the criticism of the conflict model which addresses the negative aspects of professionalism, are necessary if family therapy is to come to grips with its role in society.

Professions are communities of practitioners who as a community share certain characteristics. William Goode ascribes to a profession the following communal characteristics:

> (1) Its members are bound by a sense of identity. (2) Once in it, few leave, so that it is a terminal or continuing status for the most part. (3) Its members share values in common. (4) Its role definitions vis-à-vis both members and non-members. (5) Within areas of communal actions there is a common language, which is understood only partially by outsiders. (6) The community has power over its members. (7) Its limits are reasonably clear, though they are not physical or geographical, but social. (8) Although it does not produce the next generation biologically, it does so socially through its control over the selection of professional trainees, and through its training processes it sends these recruits through an adult socialization process.[23]

Thus professions not only have ideologies, but also possess certain characteristics of a community. Some of the concepts we use in describing our professions have quasi-religious overtones. The word "profession" etymologically

---

[23]Goode, William. "Community Within a Community." *American Sociological Review* XXII (1957): 194.

means "to testify on behalf of" or "to stand for something." The word "vocation" or "calling" has a long religious history. People are "called" to serve the community. One's vocation comes from God and one is "called" to serve the common good. We believe in the principles of marriage and family therapy. (There is obvious debate as to which principles are fundamental.) We have trust and faith in our discipline.

In contrast, the root of the word "career" refers to movement to get off and running. The word "car" and "career" come from the same root. A car is essentially a private mode of transportation.

To view our profession only in terms of a career is to adopt a myopic view of what we do. A careerist thinks privately, even in public places.[24] Our careers as family therapists are an important focus as long as we do not lose sight of what we work toward. A professional is at the same time a citizen of our society.

Reflection on the ideological assumption of our profession is difficult in that family therapy is an emerging profession. In addition, many marriage and family therapists have identities as members of other professions: medicine, psychology, social work, and the ministry. We need to be both clear and self-critical of our professional ideological assumptions as well as committed to an examination of our role in society. What do we as marriage and family therapists stand for?

---

[24]May, William. "The Beleaguered Rulers: The Public Obligations of the Professionals." *Institute of Ethics Journal* 2 (1992): 31.

VISION

Marriage and family therapy needs to have a clear vision of itself as a profession. The purpose of this book is to elucidate the moral dimensions of that vision. Stanley Hauerwas has argued for the centrality of story and vision in the moral life. For Hauerwas moral behavior is an affair not primarily of choice but of vision.[25] Eric Mount in *Professional Ethics in Context* clarifies just how deep an impact that one's vision can have:

> There was a moment in the 1988 presidential campaign when similar diversities of outlook emerged in stark opposition. During the debate between the vice presidential candidates, Senators Bentsen and Quayle were asked to recall an especially formative experience in their personal development. Speaking first, Senator Quayle recounted the advice that his grandmother, Martha Pulliom, had given to him when he was a boy: 'You can do anything you want to, if you just set your mind to it and go to work.' When his turn came Senator Bentsen recalled growing up near the Mexican border and seeing the poverty and educational needs of the Mexican-Americans. Both men were born to privilege, and both strove to capitalize on what they had received, but one man's philosophy centered on climbing the ladder of success, while the other man concerned himself with the rungs that were missing on the ladders of others. Both focused on the American dream, a powerful expression of our societal values. But they viewed the dream differently; as a result, they saw other things differently.[26]

To become a marriage and family therapist is to alter one's story and deeply affect one's vision of life.

Within this vision three dimensions have emerged in this chapter that are of critical importance. The first is the necessity for a critical analysis and reflection on our professions' role in society, ideological assumptions, and communal

---

[25]Hauerwas, Stanley. *Vision and Virtue*. Notre Dame, Indiana: Fides Publishers, 1974.

[26]Mount, Eric. *Professional Ethics in Context*. Louisville: Westminster/John Knox Press, 1990, 14–15.

characteristics. The second area of critical importance is breaking out of our middle and upper class bounds to work individually and collectively toward a balance of power in relationships and society best described as justice. We need to be about the business of liberating people from oppressive social structures. This involves working to liberate people from prejudicial attitudes and striving to overcome the bifurcation of life into private and public realms.

> Metaphysicians like Plato and Marx thought they could show that once philosophical theory had led us from appearance to reality we would be into a better position to be useful to our fellow human beings. They both hoped that the public-private split, the distinction between duty to self and duty to others could be overcome.[27]

Finally, we need to be aware of the wider contexts in which we live and work. This chapter has made a case for understanding the relationship between our profession and the society in which we live. Yet we live in a world of many cultures and nations and we live in a world in the midst of a global environmental crisis.

Case
A family is in therapy for discipline issues with their children. The father works as a high level manager for a manufacturing company that uses toxic chemicals. The man, as an aside, talks about his stress at work and how he works hard at saving his company money by circumventing environmental regulations.

How does the therapist address this important issue which is not the focus of the therapy?

---

[27]Rorty, Richard. *Contingency, Irony, and Solidarity*. New York: Cambridge University, 1989, 120.

Chapter 2
Ethical Issues Specific to Marriage and Family Therapy

After having examined the wider contexts of the issues arising in marriage and family therapy, it is time to turn to the specific issues facing practitioners. In Veatch's model of a triple contract, we turn now to focus on the third contract, i.e., between the practitioner and the client. This is where marriage and family therapy has traditionally concentrated its efforts.

AAMFT CODE OF ETHICS

The American Association of Marriage and Family Therapists' Code of Ethics describes eight areas of responsibility that can be incorporated in a code of ethics:[1]

1. Responsibility to clients
2. Confidentiality
3. Professional competence and integrity
4. Responsibility to students, employees, and supervisees
5. Responsibility to research participants
6. Responsibility to the profession
7. Financial arrangements
8. Advertising

The code spells out specific responsibilities to clients which include non-discrimination according to race, sex, or ethnic group, avoiding dual relationships (where a client has an additional relationship on a business, professional, or personal basis with the therapist), making clear that a decision on marital status is

---

[1]*Code of Ethical Principles for Marriage and Family Therapists.* The American Association of Marriage and Family Therapists, 1991.

the responsibility of the clients, not continuing the process after it is clear that the clients are no longer benefiting from it, and not abandoning clients.

Confidentiality is another area of responsibility to our clients. Confidentiality is not, however, an absolute value in that family therapists have a duty to warn of impending harm and a duty to report physical and sexual abuse of children. Family therapists have a responsibility to obtain informed consent before conferring with colleagues and other professionals. Confidentiality is different and more complicated for family therapists in that our clients are usually a couple or an entire family.

The code also describes professional competence. Competence is lost whenever the therapist is impaired in any way that interferes with the therapeutic process. Competence involves continuing education and learning about new developments in the field of family therapy. Family therapists have a responsibility not to attempt a diagnosis or treat problems outside the boundaries of family therapy.

The remaining five areas of the code describe responsibilities in the various aspects of our profession. The key themes running through these areas are responsibility and honesty. Family therapists are clear and honest in their financial contracts with clients and do not charge excessive fees (which is not specified in the code) and do not receive a payment for referrals. Family therapists do not advertise in dishonest or deceptive ways exaggerating the effectiveness of their skills and treatment processes. Family therapists respect the dignity of clients participating in research studies. Family therapists are accountable to their colleagues and to the profession. A specific section of the Code (number five) spells out this responsibility to students and supervisors entering the profession.

The responsibilities identified in the code can be further understood, although in a negative way, by looking at the types of complaints lodged against therapists in general.

Complaints against therapists fall into five major categories.[2] Three of these apply to the first area of the code: responsibility to clients. The first type of complaint occurs when therapists *exploit* clients. This happens in a number of ways: charging excessive fees, deceiving clients about themselves and the therapeutic process, and having sexual affairs with clients. Essentially, this category involves the misuse of the therapist's power and an abuse of the fiduciary (trust-based) nature of the relationship.

The next category is *insensitivity* to clients. The nature of therapeutic (healing) work with clients involves sensitivity to the needs, feelings, and rights (e.g., to be respected) of clients. Vulgar language, verbally abusive behavior, defensive and negative attitudes, are all harmful to the clients. Spending most of the session typing notes into a computer is but one example of insensitive behavior to a client.

The third category of complaints involves *abandonment*, which occurs when a therapist rejects clients who need further treatment without giving the clients adequate time to deal with the end of therapy and without giving the client appropriate referral options. Therapists have a responsibility to refer when they are unable to continue to work with clients.

---

[2]Keith-Spregel, Patricia and Gerald P. Koocher. *Ethics in Psychology: Professional Standards and Cases.* New York: Random House, 1985, 29–30.

The last two types of complaints relate primarily to the third principle of the code, professional competence and integrity. The fourth category is *incompetence*, which occurs when a clinician practices in an inadequate way or practices beyond the limits of his or her professional skills, abilities, and knowledge. Examples include inadequate diagnosis and treatment, failure to plan treatment and set goals with clients, providing services while under too much stress and too great a work load, and failing to consider other factors involved in client symptoms. An example is failing to refer a client for a medical examination when the client continues to complain of severe headaches. Family therapists are cognizant of their own as well as their professions' boundaries and work with other health-related professions for the well-being of clients.

The final category is *irresponsibility*. This includes failure to reliably and responsibly perform one's professional duties (consistently being late for appointments and not showing up for appointments) blaming others for one's mistakes, sloppy work, and excessive delays in delivering services and reports, and failing to return client phone calls.

LIMITATIONS OF CODES OF ETHICS

There is a tendency, however, for codes of ethics to be both retrospective and negative. This occurs because ethics committees first deal with complaints and then revise their codes. Codes, therefore, are examples of what moral philosophers call "quandary ethics," because they arise from the specific issues in clinical practice and lack a clear grounding in ethical theory. An example of quandary ethics is Nancy Ratliff's *A Workbook for Ethical Decision Making*, which examines dilemmas that arise in clinical practice, yet does not state or reflect on ethical assumptions, principles and theories[3].

Codes of ethics also tend to be concrete and specific; and they easily become too narrow and limited. From this narrowness some clinicians assume that a practice is okay if it is not prohibited in the code. The AAMFT code, for example, prohibits sexual relationships with a client for two years after the end of therapy. This prohibition is designed to prevent a therapeutic relationship from evolving into a sexual affair. Yet the two year time limit implies that a sexual relationship is acceptable after the time limit.

Another example of a "legislative" approach which oversimplifies the issue involved is the code's exhortation to avoid dual relationships that "could impair their professional judgment or increase the risk of exploitation."[4] Robert Ryder and Jeri Hepworth point out that dual relationships is a broad, complex, and ambiguous area that cannot simply be eliminated by a blanket of prohibition.[5] In the next section of this chapter I will examine examples of dual relationships that are positive for the client.

Another limitation of the code is that it does not examine the wider social, political, and economic contexts in which we work. The code does not consider the social contract between family therapy and our society. It does not consider the

---

[3]Ratliff, Nancy. *A Workbook for Ethical Decision Making.* El Paso: Montgomery Methods, 1988.

[4]*Code of Ethics.* American Association of Marriage and Family Therapists, Washington, D.C., 1991, 4: 1.

[5]Ryder, Robert and Jeri Hepworth. "AAMFT Ethical Code: 'Dual Relationships'." *Journal of Marital and Family Therapy* 16 (1990): 127–132.

issue raised in the first chapter of a profession's charter. The code does not deal with justice and environmental issues. In the next chapter I will address the duties that family therapists have as citizens in the contemporary world.

The next limitation is that the code attempts to deal with the economic dimension by means of the principles of honesty and fairness. Professions in our society have a "trade" or business dimension. Professional organizations get complaints when the economic dimension overrides or interferes with the therapeutic dimension. There are two clear examples of the economic dimension interfering with clinical judgment. The first example is pretending to do therapy but without any actual therapeutic work being done. The rationale offered by some clinicians is that this is okay as long as no unprofessional conduct occurs and clients pay their fees. In this sense therapy becomes the purchase of a friendship. The second example is failing to bring therapy to an end. Therapists don't like unemployment and tend to avoid actions which would end therapy. The economic dimension needs to be examined and analyzed within the primary context of the therapeutic relationship. With the complexity issues involved, it is clearly beyond the scope of a code of ethics to adequately examine the economic dimension of clinical practice.

The final limitation of the AAMFT Code of Ethics involves the issue of clarifying the boundaries of a therapeutic relationship. Within AAMFT there is a consensus that the therapeutic relationship needs clear boundaries. A person calls for an appointment. The therapist assumes the initial appointment is for assessing whether or not therapy is appropriate (and with whom). The client, however, assumes that he or she has a therapist by virtue of the call. A client angrily terminates therapy and feels that it has ended. The therapist, however, has a responsibility to make recommendations and referrals for help in the future. In this sense the therapy is not over until this communication is sent and received.

Another aspect of this boundary issue concerns coverage for absences on the part of the therapist. The next dimension revolves around availability and accessibility. There are many ways in which therapists can be accessible to their clients. Also, therapists work in a wide variety of contexts ranging from private practice to working for state and federal government agencies. My argument based upon the above examples and considerations is that while there is a consensus that good therapy involves good boundaries the issue is far too complex to be resolved within the confines of a code of ethics. Codes have the limitations I have discussed and yet are useful as starting points for the issues facing marriage and family therapists.

NONSEXUAL DUAL RELATIONSHIPS

The AAMFT Code of Ethics addresses the issue of dual relationships under paragraph 1.2 "Responsibility to Clients" and paragraph 4.1 "Responsibility to Students, Employees, and Supervisors."

> Paragraph 1.2: Marriage and family therapists are cognizant of their influential position with respect to clients, and they avoid exploiting the trust and dependence of such persons. Therapists, therefore, make every effort to avoid dual relationships with clients that could impair their professional judgment or increase the risk of exploitation. When a dual relationship cannot be avoided, therapists take appropriate professional precautions to inspire so judgment is not impaired and no exploitation occurs. Examples of such dual relationships include, but are not limited to, business or close personal relationships with clients.

Section 4:1 of the Code adds, "…with students, employees, or supervisees."

There are four basic arguments against dual relationships. The first and most compelling is that the client is put at risk. In dual relationships there is a greater chance that the client could be exploited and treated unfairly. Being a client in a therapeutic relationship involves vulnerability, and the client therefore cannot enter another relationship on an equal footing.

The second argument against dual relationships is that with two relationships the boundary issues become more complex. Conflicts in one relationship can spill over and affect the other relationship.

The next argument is that a therapist being involved in a dual relationship could have his or her objectivity and impartiality impaired. A therapist who experiences uncomfortable feelings as a result of a conflict in a business relationship could begin to distance himself or herself from the client in the therapeutic process.

The final argument against dual relationships revolves around a worst case scenario. Therapists could begin to use their practices as a screening device to find business partners, consultants, other professional services, and even as a dating service after the two year statute of limitations.

All of the above arguments have a common thread, i.e., dual relationships "could impair" the therapeutic relationship. Clearly, empirical research is needed, otherwise the assumption is that "could" means "probably" or "will."

There are three arguments in favor of dual relationships. Dual relationships are common particularly where there is a college or university near where the practitioner works. I have personally avoided dual relationships involving therapy with students because the client/student in a dual relationship involves an unequal hierarchy. Last summer a student in my course called in a state of shock because her husband had drowned in a whitewater rafting accident. The student wanted, and needed, help with her grief and selected me for two reasons: first, she knew me; and, second, one of my hobbies is whitewater rafting. After explaining the nature of dual relationships, I decided to do the therapy my student had requested. The dual relationship existed for two months while I was teaching the course. The therapy continued for seven months. In this particular case the dual relationship was beneficial. As a general practice, I continue to avoid doing therapy with students, but this experience has opened up for me the idea that in some cases dual relationships are positive. To avoid such relationships because they "could" produce negative consequences is to avoid dealing with the complex issues involved.

The second argument for dual relationships is that in working closely together people develop friendships. This is particularly true in agencies in the early stages of growth and development. Agencies become our "work families" and when we are involved in healthy relationships it is natural to want to socialize outside the workplace. It is both inappropriate and a waste of effort to prohibit such friendships. This issue changes as organizations become larger and more structured. As the executive director of a large (staff of 35) pastoral counseling agency, I now no longer cultivate personal friendship with colleagues because of the size of the agency and because I am committed to treating all of my employees' fairly. This is not to say that other people on the staff might not develop close personal friendships.

The third argument is that many family therapists have other professional roles in the community. I am both a marriage and family therapist and a chaplain in a nearby National Guard unit. In the last seven years many Guardsmen have come to me with their family problems. Many of them have been reluctant to enter therapy. As a chaplain, I have persuaded many of them to seek therapeutic assistance for their problems. I give them a variety of referral possibilities. In two out of three cases they decide to enter therapy with me. In the first session I explain the nature and possible problems with dual relationships. In all but one case (which I referred because of complications that arose) the outcome of the therapy was successful and was enhanced by my additional role as chaplain. My experience is an example of where dual relationships enhance the therapy rather than complicate it. Research needs to be done on the many different types of dual relationships and which ones tend to work.

Ryder and Hepworth in their analyses of dual relationships point out that in situations where the client is not put at risk and the relationship is mutually beneficial, that they are morally acceptable.[6]

Our examination of the arguments for and against dual relationships demonstrates the benefits as well as the changes and shows how complex the issue is for practitioners. As I have concluded in the previous section of this chapter a statement or principle in a code cannot deal with the issue in a comprehensive and balanced way.

---

[6]*ibid.*, 130.

DILEMMAS

In the practice of marriage and family therapy practitioners constantly face

dilemmas. Current literature in marriage and family therapy considers the ethical

dilemmas that clinicians face, both those considered in the Code of Ethics and those

outside it. Nancy Ratliff, in her book *A Workbook for Ethical Decision Making*,[7] as

well as Susan Green and James Hansen, in their article "Ethical Dilemmas Faced by

Family Therapists"[8] (*Journal of Marriage and Family Therapy*) both identify several

---

[7]Ratliff, Nancy. *A Workbook for Ethical Decision Making*. El Paso: Montgomery Methods, 1988, 16.
1. Reporting child abuse
2. Warning another party of potential harm
3. Issues involving fees
4. Unethical conduct by another professional
5. Nonsexual relationships with former clients
6. Working with minors without parental consent
7. Confidentiality with multiple family members
8. Advertising
9. Confidentiality with a third party contractor
10. Reporting crimes
11. Sexual behavior with clients
12. Forensic testimony
13. Testimony in child custody
14. Supervisor/supervisee relationship
15. Practicing in area beyond competence
16. Abuse of prescription drugs
17. Consultation and conflict of interest
18. Endorsement of products
19. Public media advice
20. Failure to inform of adjunctive treatment (e.g., AA)
21. Inappropriate hospitalization of clients
22. Procedure of ethics committee (reports)
23. Confidentiality in staffing and presentations
24. Client reports dissatisfaction with other therapists
25. Suicide threats

[8]Green, Susan and James Hansen. "Ethical Dilemmas Faced by Family Therapists." *Journal of Marriage and Family Therapy* 2 (1989): 149–158.
1. Treating the entire family
2. Differing therapist and family values
3. Treating entire family after one member leaves
4. Professional development activities
5. Imposing therapist's values
6. Integrity (manipulating family for therapeutic benefit)
7. Payment for services
8. Decisions on marital status

dozen dilemmas. My purpose, at this point, is not to deal with these specific dilemmas, but rather to identify those fundamental areas which underlie the issues we encounter in practicing marriage and family therapy.

The first area that generates dilemmas is the variety of ethnic, cultural, and religious values found in our pluralistic society. Families live in the context of these complex value systems. What is required of us is not so much knowledge of each specific value system, though that can be helpful, but sensitivity to these value systems and how they impact on the lives and relationships of our clients. Some of these value systems are religious in nature and can face us with challenging dilemmas.

Case

A couple requests family therapy because of the behavior problems of their ten-year-old son. After the sixth session the boy becomes ill and is hospitalized. The physicians say an operation is necessary. The parents, based on their religious beliefs, refuse to allow a blood transfusion.

In this case the therapist feels that these religious beliefs are both wrong and harmful. The dilemma here is: "Can the clinician continue to work with the family given the fundamental differences in the values and beliefs of therapist and client?" The dilemma needs to be considered from both sides. The family's comfort level with these value differences is a crucial factor. Equally important are the feelings of

---

9. Reporting child abuse
10. Supervision of trainees
11. Family vs. individual needs
12. Consultation with other professionals
13. Informed consent
14. Testifying
15. Unethical organizations
16. Sharing research results

the therapist. Clearly, a therapist is obligated to refer clients when the differences in

value systems makes therapy difficult or impossible.

A second underlying area involves gender values and gender roles. This

domain is difficult in that it is a part of the history of each one of us, and only

relatively recently have we become aware of its profound and pervasive impact.

Case
A couple in their thirties comes in for marriage counseling. As they describe their issues the woman says that we should talk about the "F" word (by which she means "Feminism"). The couple want help on a number of issues as well as help in coming to grips in their marriage with the value tensions introduced by the woman's feminist values.

In this case I don't believe that the marital therapist must be a feminist. This

might not even be advisable in that it would alienate the man. What is required of

the therapist is an openness to feminist thought and values. Since we live in the first

generation to uncover the influence of gender roles, complete and objective

knowledge is impossible. But, here again, sensitivity must be the basis of the

therapist's attitudes toward this aspect of our lives and our relationships.

The final area of our practice that generates dilemmas is the basic tension

between the individual and the marriage or the family. This is of both clinical and

ethical concern for us as family therapists. Michael Nichols, in his book *The Self in*

the System, thoroughly explores the tension between the individual and the family.[9]

The following case illustrates an ethical dilemma arising from this tension.

Case
A twenty-nine-year-old woman presents herself for therapy. She is depressed and states that she wants to end her marriage. The couple has two preschool age children. The woman belongs to a support group that is

---

[9]Nichols, Michael. *The Self in the System: Expanding the Limits of Family Therapy*. New York: Brunner Mazel, 1987.

led by a feminist colleague. To work with the woman is to embark on a growth process that will in all likelihood end in a divorce. Does the therapist go with individual therapy or push to see the couple to determine if there is any possibility of improving the marriage? If the marriage improves, perhaps her depression will lift. Can the therapist help her to grow within the context of the marriage? How much influence should the therapist bring to bear and in what direction?

In this case we have a "format of treatment" dilemma and an ethical dilemma at one and the same time. Clearly the direction in which the therapist pushes will in all likelihood be an important influence on both the woman's and the couple's decision about the future of their marriage.

Another ethical issue within this area involves family therapists who refuse treatment unless the whole family participates. We have all encountered individuals and family subsystems who don't want their part of the system treated. In some families older children are now young adults and have successfully negotiated healthy distances from their family of origin. In these situations family therapy could be emotionally regressive and harmful.

Individual issues tend to revolve around well-being and self-esteem, while marital and family issues oscillate around conflicts of interest and justice issues. There is a tension we all experience between our needs to be separate individuals and our togetherness needs which we meet in our marriages and families. As family therapists we work with this fundamental tension in human life.

PARADOXICAL THERAPY

Another issue, not in the AAMFT Code of Ethics, that needs to be addressed is the issue of the use of paradoxical techniques in family therapy. The techniques of paradoxical therapy are now well known in our field. These techniques involve the manipulation of a person outside of that person's awareness in order to change a frame of reference or behavior. Paradoxical techniques are based upon a deceitful stance from which the therapist manipulates. Jay Haley argues that as long as the therapist has the client's best interests at heart that ethical issues should take a back seat.[10] Therapists are often afraid that if clients know about the techniques of therapy they will render the therapy ineffective. Paradoxical techniques contribute to the power and mystique of the therapist.

I maintain that clients have the right to know about both the therapy and techniques that are being used. This right is important in that it gives clients the freedom to choose to participate or not. Clients' right to know is grounded in a "respect for persons" ethical principle which will be developed in the next chapter. A consideration of the techniques of paradoxical therapy leads to an examination of how belief systems function in the minds and practices of family therapists.

BELIEF SYSTEMS

Belief systems are another crucial aspect of our work as family therapists that are beyond the scope of the AAMFT Code of Ethics. Three aspects of our belief systems need to be examined.

Research in family therapy has highlighted the role of belief systems in the families that come to us for treatment. The Bowen approach to family therapy has

---

[10]Henderson, Michael C. "Paradoxical Process and Ethical Consciousness." *Family Therapy* 3 (1987): 191. See also: Haley, J. *Problem-Solving Therapy*. 2nd ed., San Francisco: Jossey-Bass, 1987, 218–243. Abate, Luciano L. and Gerald R. Weeks. "Professional and Ethical Issues." In *Paradoxical Psychotherapy*. New York: Brunner Mazel, 1982, Chapter 12.

emphasized the importance of the therapist dealing with his or her own family of origin and its attendant belief systems. Every time we see a couple or family we bring our belief systems about the nature of marriages and families into the room with us. In considering our own belief systems, a fundamental question for therapists arises: Do we regard our own belief systems as factual (objective) truths or do we see them as subjective truths by which we live? Soren Kierkegaard, the nineteenth century Danish philosopher, led philosophy to recognize the subjective nature of truth. Kierkegaard regarded "truth" as both subjective and plural; thereby rejecting an underlying assumption long held in Western philosophy that there is a single, objective truth that we are trying to discover and align ourselves with. Kierkegaard also distinguished between truth and passion for truth (truthfulness). Thus, he could admire Socrates' passion for truth while rejecting certain objective aspects of his philosophy. I maintain that it is essential for family therapists to respect (not to agree with) the belief systems of clients. If we assume our belief systems are true while judging our clients belief systems as false, we impede our ability to empathize with them and enter into their worlds in helpful ways. Within our field of family therapy we have the best example of multiple versions of the truth with the various approaches to family therapy. We tend to affiliate with those theories of the family and of family therapy that are congruent with our own belief systems. Consequently, we must be alert to learn about our clients and colleagues experiences which are not part of our own belief system. Belief systems help us make sense out of our lives and our relationships. At the same time we are all limited by the boundaries of our own belief systems.

Another important aspect of our belief systems are those concepts which interfere with the moral dimension of our work. We must look continually at our own idealism. Attachment to our own idealism can prevent us from examining the realities of our work as well as looking at the "shadow" side of professional life. Another belief that prevents any examination of the moral dimension of family therapy is the idea that therapy is a scientifically based technology that is value free. Another belief that can interfere is the idea that ethics is merely adherence to administrative and legal standards. Variations of this are beliefs that ethics is a matter of customs and practices and that ethics is simply following the rules of one's professional association.

The third aspect of our belief systems is the most difficult to critically evaluate. It is our professional "corporate" beliefs. These beliefs are in fact assumptions which make up our world-view. It is not surprising that other professions do a better job at examining. Magali Larson, a sociologist, identifies four basic elements in our professional ideologies which are, in fact, inaccurate when compared to the current ways in which professionals function in our society.[11]

The first element is that professionals see themselves oriented to service rather than profit. The reality, however, is that professionals generally pursue high socioeconomic status and tend to serve the middle and upper class. Thus, there is a distinctly self-serving aspect to the way in which we practice our professions. The second element justifies economic and status rewards on the basis of superior skills

---

[11]Larson, Magali. *The Rise of Professionalism.* Berkeley CA: University of California Press, 1977, 412–416.

and abilities, ignoring the fact that the route to this privileged position is through our educational systems which are provided by our society. Thus, our justification does not consider our "charter" by society. The third element of our corporate ideology is that we have elevated professional work above non-professional, thus establishing a social distance between professionals and other workers. This in part accounts for the phenomenon now that everyone wants to become a professional. The final element of our corporate ideologies is that professions see themselves as subscribing to a superior ethic of service which makes us trustworthy to manage a monopoly of services vital to our society. Here the animating belief is that professions contribute maximally and efficiently to human welfare.

Family therapists participate in the professional ideologies prevalent in our society. We need to critically examine the distances between our ideals and the realities of our practices and the socioeconomic realities of our society. This analysis of our corporate belief systems and ideologies needs to occur within the profession of marriage and family therapy (and from without with the help of sociologists, philosophers, and other disciplines).

DIAGNOSIS AND THE THERAPEUTIC CONTRACT

The last area within marriage and family therapy that gives rise to ethical issues is the related issue of diagnosis and the therapeutic contract. Carl Whitaker maintains that two struggles or battles occur in the beginning of the therapeutic process.[12] The first is the battle for structure, which involves the frequency of

---

[12]Neill, John R. *From Psyche to System: The Evolving Therapy of Carl Whitaker*. ed. David Kniskein. New York: Guilford Press, 1982.

sessions, who attends, the fee, and other contractual aspects of the therapy. The second battle, according to Whitaker, revolves around who is responsible for change. The therapist must lose this battle in that changes in feelings, attitudes and ways of relating are the responsibility of clients. Whitaker sees the therapist as a catalyst in the process of change. These two battles—the first of which should be won by the therapist, the second of which should be won by the client—forms the basis for the therapeutic contract. Carol Anderson points out that a great many issues in therapy stem from either lack of clarity in, or difficulties in, the therapeutic contract.[13] For example, clients who feel that they were not treated fairly in the contracting phase tend to express themselves by dropping out of the process. Fairness issues that surface at this point indicate that the ethical dimensions of the therapeutic contract have not been adequately dealt with. A mutually acceptable contract goes a long way in forming a good relationship.

The initial phase of therapy not only involves contracting, but also focuses on diagnosis. Diagnosis has developed in medical and psychiatric contexts. This focus continues to this day in that the DSMIII-R does not include "relational" categories of diagnosis. This omission is not surprising given marital therapy has long been a practice in search of a theory. (A recent exception is Ellyn Bader and Peter Pearson's book, *In Quest of the Mythical Mate: A Developmental Approach to Diagnosis and Treatment in Couples Therapy*.[14]) Diagnosis is critical in the

---

[13]Anderson, Carol. *The Therapeutic Contract*. Family Therapy Network Symposium, Washington, D.C., 1987.

[14]Bader, Ellyn and Peter Pearson. *In Quest of the Mythical Mate: A Developmental Approach to Diagnosis and Treatment in Couples Therapy*. New York: Brunner Mazel, 1988.

therapeutic process in that it involves the clinician's understanding of the clients and their problems.

Another common ethical problem in the area of diagnosis is insurance fraud. It is always unethical for a clinician signing an insurance form to misrepresent the facts regarding the services rendered (e.g., date and length of sessions). The most obvious case is a supervisor as the primary therapist who has actually had little or no contact with the client signing the form. Therapists or supervisors knowing their role in the treatment have not put it on the insurance form arguing that there was no description of their role (as a consultant to the therapist, for example) on the form. The AAMFT Commission on Supervision recommends writing the appropriate information on the form if it does not appear there.

This issue of insurance fraud for marriage and family therapists is complicated by the fact that the DSMIII-R has been developed by the psychiatric profession. The psychiatric profession's model is individualistic (as opposed to relationships) and views pathology in intrapsychic terms (focuses on what is wrong rather than evoking possibilities). Thus there is a clear difference in basic assumptions between psychiatry and marriage and family therapy. The conflict on a political level is between an established profession and an emerging one. My point is that differences in orientation do not give ethical grounds for distorting the facts about the services rendered.

Edwin Friedman argues that family therapy is a matter of theoretical orientation that does not revolve around the number of people in the session. Thus Friedman does his version of Bowen's family of origin work with one person in the therapy session. This leads us into a common gray area. Since most insurance companies do not cover either marriage or family therapy, many clinicians work out with a couple, for example, which one of them is to be diagnosed in DSMIII-R categories. On the insurance form it appears that one person is being treated for an individual symptom. In actuality the therapist is doing marital therapy which focuses on treating the relationship. Again we are confronted with differing viewpoints. Not only do disciplines see the issues quite differently but also with the field of family therapy some therapists regard issues as treatment matters while others see the same issue in ethical terms. The most common example of this is the issue of who (what members of the family) to involve in treatment. Since who is in the therapeutic process may have a profound impact on decisions made about children or even the future of the marriage, I maintain that treatment issues and moral issues are coextensive and that both must be considered in doing family therapy.

A final issue arises from the contract and diagnosis areas—the issue of limits. Michael Bayles, in "Ethics of Limited Knowledge in the Healing Professions," points out that professionals do not bear the consequences of their judgments and decisions.[15] Our current knowledge is at best provisional, representing only what is known in family therapy at the present. It is necessarily partial and incomplete. Moreover, family therapy interacts with the fields of psychology, medicine, and psychiatry, whose concepts and methods are provisional also. All of the health-related professions are attempting to help people on the basis of what is currently

---

[15]Bayles, Michael D. "Ethics of Limited Knowledge in the Healing Professions." In *Professional Ethics in Health Care Services*, ed. Eugene Kelly. New York: University Press of America, 1988.

known. For these reasons a critical requirement is to be aware of and recognize the *limits* of our current knowledge. Otherwise, we will be guilty of what the Greeks described as "hubris," the sin of pride in going beyond our limits. This is a basic temptation not only in family therapy but in all the professions in that we function within the "expert" role with our clients on a daily basis. We can easily be seduced by our own knowledge. Being aware of the limits of our knowledge and skills is the best way to avoid falling into the trap of hubris.

CONCLUSION

I began this chapter with a look at the AAMFT Code of Ethics. While the code provides a clear set of guidelines, the issues currently facing family therapy go beyond the limitations of the code. Our investigation into the current literature on ethical issues in marriage and family therapy has brought us to several conclusions. Three requirements for marriage and family therapists seem clear after looking at the current issues. The first is our obligation to be sensitive to the fundamental dilemmas in our field. A second requirement is to recognize the relativity of our belief systems and theories. Our third obligation is to be aware of the ethical dimensions of the therapeutic contract.

An additional question emerges. Are the issues raised in marriage and family therapy such that unique moral principles are required? Alan Goldman argues that strongly differentiated professions (law, for example, with its commitment that even the worst criminal is deserving of a good legal defense) require a unique set of moral principles that apply specifically to that profession.[16] But this does not seem so in the field of marriage and family therapy. Rather, Robert Veatch's position, that there is no such thing as "professional ethics," but only ethical principles applied to a specific professional context, is a more reasonable position.

I have described the basic dilemmas and issues in the field of marriage and family therapy. While these dilemmas will always be with us, it is important that we move beyond mere dilemma ethics to basic principles that will inform our work. Christina Sommers maintains that some things are clearly right and some are clearly wrong and that there are some ethical truths that are not subject to serious debate. Sommers states that..."it is wrong to mistreat a child, to humiliate someone, to torment an animal. To think only of yourself, to steal, to lie, to break promises. And on the positive side: it is right to be considerate and respectful of others, to be charitable and generous."[17]

In addition to such very basic ethical truths, we can find help in understanding how we assimilate conceptual and ethical knowledge. William Perry, investigating intellectual and ethical development in college students, postulates three stages in the assimilation of new knowledge. The first stage is dualism in which the categories are right and wrong. The search is for the right answer to the ethical question. The second stage is multiplicity which concludes that there are as many truths as there are people. This stage involves subjectivism and leads to frustration and ethical relativism. Since all perspectives are equally valid, there is no basis for

---

[16]Goldman, Alan H. *The Moral Foundations of Professional Ethics.* Totowa NJ: Roman and Littlefield, 1980.

[17]Sommers, Christina. "Teaching the Virtues." *American Philosophical Newsletter,* 1991, 42.

commitment. From this frustration emerges the third stage, contextual relativism. This stage involves an awareness of the role of contexts in shaping values and truth. A diversity of perspectives is recognized and appreciated yet a commitment to principles and critical analysis guides a person's thoughts and actions.[18]

Marital and family therapy needs to be viewed from start to finish as a moral activity. The practice of marriage and family therapy provides us with a unique context in which to wrestle with reoccurring human issues. In the following chapters I will apply four distinct approaches to moral philosophy (duty-based, rights-based, developmental, and virtue-based) to the work of the marriage and family therapist.

---

[18]Perry, William. *Forms of Intellectual and Ethical Development in the College Years*. New York: Holt, Rinehart, and Winston, 1970.

Chapter 3
Duties of Marriage and Family Therapists

One of the cornerstones in Western moral philosophy is the existence of a number of ethical theories which are classified as duty-based (deontological) approaches. Duty-based approaches begin ethical analyses with an investigation of a person's duties toward others. Duties can be defined as the fundamental moral obligations we have toward one another. In this chapter I will focus on examining the duties that marriage and family therapists have toward their clients and their profession. In the following chapter I will examine these duties from the perspective of the client—the issue of the rights of clients. These perspectives are interrelated in that if a client has a right to something then the therapist has a duty to provide that something. A glance at the history of ethical thinking about duties gives us a better understanding of what duties are and are not.

KANT

Immanuel Kant (1724–1804), the German philosopher, is the founder of the duty-based approach to ethics. Kant's moral philosophy is built on three basic principles. The first is that we have a fundamental duty to act out of a sense of good moral will toward others. Is the action I am about to perform evidence of good moral will toward the other person? Thus, stealing from a colleague does not show good moral will. The second principle is Kant's categorical imperative which provides an objective criterion for applying the basic duty of good moral will. The categorical imperative states that I must be able to will that the implied rule of my action become a universal law. I cannot treat myself and my actions as exceptions (i.e., as categories of one). If my action is right, according to Kant, I must be able to predicate my action into a universal practice. This is how Kant moves from self to others in his moral philosophy. The final principle is Kant's idea that we must treat others as ends and not as means. This is described as Kant's "respect for persons" principle. My duty is to show this respect for persons in my attitudes and actions involving others. Kant's overall contribution to moral philosophy is his insistence on impartiality, i.e., on the need for universal application of moral principles.[1]

UPWARD AND DOWNWARD APPROACHES TO ETHICAL THEORIES

Henri Bergson (1859–1941), the French philosopher, helps us understand what duties are because he pointed out that ethical theories tend to flow in two directions.[2] Bergson describes ethical theories which move in the direction of aspiration (for example, Aristotle with his vision of the good life). The other direction is with ethical theories which focus on the duties we have toward one another. (Kant's approach is the prime example here.) Bergson's distinction is useful in helping us understand ethical theories which originate in different religions. Roman Catholic moral theology, for instance, involves aspiration, i.e., it

---

[1]Kant, Immanuel. *Groundwork of the Metaphysic of Morals.* Translated by H. J. Paton, New York: Harper & Row, 1964.

[2]Cusa, A. S. *Dimensions of Moral Creativity.* University Park: The Pennsylvania State University Press, 1978, 46.

is goal-centered (teleological). Thus ethics, from this perspective, needs to be done in the context of the meaning and purpose of our lives, which can only be done when we consider our divine origins. In contrast, Protestant thought, with its shift toward a "work ethic," moves toward a here and now focus on one's duties (deontological). Allan Dyer has clearly delineated the differences in these two approaches:[3]

Upward Perspective	Downward Perspective
moral inspiration	regulation of abuse
affective	cognitive
self-reflective	critical
post-critical	analytical
teleological (end and goal-based)	deontological (rule-based)
fiduciary relationships	adversarial relationships
based on trust	based on control
tacit	explicit

KITCHENER'S APPROACH

K. S. Kitchener has developed an approach to ethics which blends clinical work with ethical theory. Kitchener's approach begins with two premises. The first is the importance of consequences and the second is "...the assumption that ethical

---

[3]Dyer, Allen. *Ethics in Psychiatry: Toward Professional Definition.* Washington D.C.: American Psychiatric Press, 1988, 48.

decisions are dependent on the situation."[4] On the basis of these premises, Kitchener operates on two levels. The first is an intuitive level which consists of a set of beliefs about what is right and wrong. Kitchener describes this intuitive set of ethical beliefs as "ordinary moral sense" which he thinks is not intrinsic or innate but developed. Ordinary moral sense depends on individual experience and it changes in the light of new experiences and new knowledge. While ordinary moral sense is limited and subjective, it nonetheless provides a basis for making ethical judgments. The ordinary moral sense interacts with the situation on an intuitive level.

For Kitchener the most important reason for not relying solely on the intuitive level is that it does not give therapists the ability to critically evaluate their decisions. The second level of his model is the critical-evaluative level which consists of ethical rules, principles, and theory. The AAMFT Code of Ethics prohibits having sex with clients (the *rule*). This is based upon a principle that to do so would violate the boundaries of a professional relationship. This principle in turn is based upon a theory (that we have a duty to respect our clients) to spell out rules and principles. Kitchener goes on to develop his own duty-based ethical theory as illustrated in Figure 1.

---

[4]Zygmond, Mary Jo and Harriet Boorhem. "Ethical Decision Making in Family Therapy." *Family Process* 28 (Sept 1989): 271.

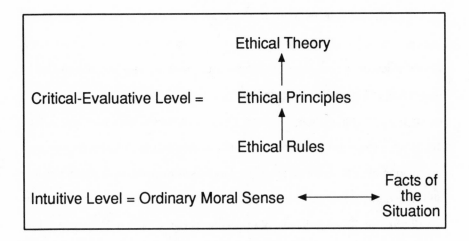

FIGURE 1: KITCHENER'S APPROACH

Kitchener uses W. D. Ross's duty-based theory. At the level of this theory Kitchener's approach has moved reflection on issues arising in clinical work to an involvement with ethical theory on a critical-evaluative level.

W. D. ROSS

The English philosopher W. D. Ross follows Kant's duty-based approach but disagrees with Kant's assumption that good results will follow if we act from good moral will. Ross goes further than Kant in developing a duty-based theory that specifies our duties. I believe that Ross's specific list of duties is more helpful to the practitioner than Kant's.[5]

---

[5]Ross, William D. *The Right and The Good.* Oxford: Clarendon Press, 1930.

Ross describes seven prima facie acts as duties. Duties based on prior acts of my own are: (1) making reparation for wrongs done, and (2) to keep promises. Duties based on the prior acts of another are: (3) duties of gratitude fulfilled by responding to those who have helped us, and (4) doing good (beneficence) helping others based on their needs. Finally, in Ross's approach, there are three general duties : (5) avoiding evil or non malfeasance, (6) the duty of justice or the equitable distribution of good and evil, and (7) a duty of self improvement. Karen Lebacqz adds two duties for doing professional work: (8) respect for a person's autonomy developed from Kant's principle of respect for persons, and (9) the duty to tell the truth.[6]

Ross's formulation of ethical duties can easily be applied to the work of marriage and family therapists. Ross's second duty of keeping promises is fundamental to the relational nature of marriage and family therapy. Only upon our fidelity to our promises and commitment can trust be built. Michael Bayles argues that the fiduciary model (trust-based) is the best basis for professional relationships.[7] Ross's fourth duty of beneficence is also at the heart of family therapy. Our reason for being therapists is helping others based on their needs. Our profession is in this sense based upon beneficence.

Ross's fifth duty of non-malfeasance is important in therapy. In our endeavor to help others, it is our basic duty to avoid harm to our clients, their self-esteem, and their relationships. Sometimes, however, we confront clients, which has the

---

[6]Lebacqz, Karen. *Professional Ethics: Power and Paradox*. Nashville: Abingdon Press, 1985, 25.

[7]Bayles, Michael. *Professional Ethics*. 2nd ed., Belmont CA: Wadsworth Publishing Co., 1989.

immediate effect of hurting their feelings, for the purpose of clarifying the destructive consequences of their ways of relating. A good example of this is an alcoholic client. As therapists we have a duty to keep a fundamental regard for our own clients and their well-being.

Ross's next duty, justice, is basic to the practice of family therapy. In our work we have a responsibility to treat our clients fairly. This involves clear contracts in the therapeutic process. The average person faces three potential problems in obtaining family therapy: the economic, ethnic, and geographical maldistribution of existing services. Marriage and family therapy grew up in a middle class environment. Significant attempts have been made to make services available to the poor and to all ethnic groups. Yet middle and upper class clients continue to make up the bulk of most of our case loads. Under the duty of justice, we have an obligation to make our therapy available to people of low incomes. This is most often done by using a sliding fee scale. Another way to provide services to those who cannot pay is to set aside a certain number of hours for pro bono services. Yet there are issues of motivation with clients that are seen at a low fee or no fee at all. Low fees tend to devaluate the services we provide. Fees are one of the prime vehicles by which clients invest and make a commitment to the therapeutic process.

The duty of justice opens the door to what has traditionally been described as "distributive justice," first identified by Aristotle as the distribution of scarce resources.[8] Considerable work has been done on this issue in the field of bioethics.

---

[8]Aristotle. *The Nichomachean Ethics*. Book V, Chapter III. Translated by J. A. K. Thompson. London: Penguin Books, 1976, 177–179.

The same issue presents itself in the distribution of marriage and family therapy resources. With this duty in mind, AAMFT, as the national professional organization, has a responsibility to advocate and bring about changes in public policy that would better distribute family therapy services. Another method of doing this would be a professional draft—requiring family therapists to serve for a period of time to work with the poorer groups in our society.

In this area an intriguing question surfaces: "Do immoral and criminal clients have the same right to therapy as everyone else?" Does a family therapist have a right to refuse treatment to these types of clients? Here again we encounter the issue of justice. As therapists we are inclined to be compassionate. A compassionate person cannot by definition be an unjust person.

Ross's seventh duty of self-improvement is especially important for the field of marriage and family therapy. The Socratic injunction of "know thyself" becomes "know thy family." In view of the constantly accelerating developments in our field, it has been suggested that in terms of content the half-life of a Ph.D. is now about ten years. Therefore, continuing education becomes a necessity.

The duties of respect for persons and truth-telling that Lebacqz adds to Ross's seven basic duties are also particularly relevant to our work as family therapists. The duty to respect persons involves both our attitude and our actions. Our responsibility is not to have certain feelings about our clients (for example, liking them), but rather to relate in respectful ways. Respect for persons overlaps with the final duty of truth-telling. It is easy to deceive our clients by withholding our thoughts and concerns. In doing therapy, however, truth-telling is not an isolated and absolute duty, rather, it is critical as to how we tell the truth to our clients. It is in how carefully we tell the truth to our clients that we give clear indication of our respect for them.

DUTIES TO THE PROFESSION

In addition to our duties toward clients, we have duties toward our profession. Our duty of respect for persons, for example, particularly applies to our profession. As family therapists it is our duty to show a basic respect for our profession and our colleagues. Evolving out of this duty is a duty to work collaboratively with our colleagues and with other professionals whose work touches ours. Our profession is but another context in which we function. The greatest number of ethical complaints about therapists comes from those working in isolation. Cooperation and not competition is our norm.

An additional duty involves our responsibility to protect others from harm even though they are not our clients. The Tarasoff case, in which a woman was murdered by a man who had told his therapist of his intent to kill Miss Tarasoff, gave rise to a clarification of our duty to warn others of impending harm. Medical ethics has long held to the basic duty of the physician to do no harm. This duty has been recast in positive terms as the *duty to protect*. We have a duty to protect both our clients and others from harm. This duty sometimes involves a painful responsibility: to report abuse that is or has been done by another professional.

Case
An attractive divorced woman comes in for therapy. The woman finds it difficult to trust you and engage in the relationship. After some time you learn that she has an ongoing affair with her former therapist, begun during her therapy with him. You know the other therapist and respect his work— and he is also single. No marriages are being disrupted by this affair, yet it is clear that your client has been emotionally harmed by the way in which

the relationship began. The woman says she wants to continue the relationship which she finds rewarding. You feel a duty to report this violation to the professional association to which both you and your therapist friend belong.

The last area of duties to the profession involves our duty to the institutions in which we work. These duties follow the general duties that employees have toward their employers. Yet in this context family therapists may also experience difficult dilemmas.

Case

A U. S. Army chaplain is a clinical member of AAMFT and works in an army post as a family life chaplain responsible for providing marriage and family therapy for soldiers and their families. A young soldier and his wife come in for both marriage and family counseling. The couple are committed to working both on their marital issues as well as issues that have come up in parenting their children. The soldier is a young captain with a promising military future. The officer has never struck his wife or children and is working to control his temper. On several occasions he has punched holes in the wall and thrown objects. You feel a duty to protect his wife and children from physical harm. At the same time you do not want to harm the officer. You have a duty to report the situation to your commanding officer, especially since the soldier has exhibited the same kind of behavior in his military training. You are caught between your duty to protect your employer, this family, and your duty not to harm this soldier.

DUTIES TO THE PUBLIC

The widest area of duties for family therapists are "the public duties."[9] There is a new awareness that all professions have obligations to society as a whole. This implied "social contract" between professionals and society requires that we serve the public interest and the common good. Public duties of professions originate with the duty of justice. We have a duty to work for a balance of power which can

---

[9] "Public Duties of the Professions." Briarcliff Manor NY: *Hastings Center Report*, 1987.

best be described as justice. As previously discussed, this involves our obligation to make our therapeutic services available to the least well-off in our society and to work toward the elimination of forms of prejudice found in ourselves, our clients, and our society.

Another aspect of our public duties is our responsibility to be good citizens of our country. This means involvement with the political arena of life as opposed to the traditional professional stance of non-involvement. Our duty to be good citizens involves also responsibility to be citizens of the world. This involves developing the ability to transcend concern for our own national boundaries. Further, this leads to our final public duty, a planetary one, the duty to lead an environmentally sound lifestyle. Family therapy has had significant positive impact on certain areas of physical and sexual abuse and this needs to be extended to forms of environmental abuse.

Clearly, all these public duties are not unique to the field of family therapy. Rather, they are essential to all professionals because they are the duties that go with being a good citizen. Albert Flores, in *Professional Ideals*, points out that there continues to be a widespread and persistent tendency to think of moral issues in individualistic terms.[10] We need to expand our ideas of professional duties to include duties to the profession and the public.

---

[10]Flores, Albert. *Professional Ideals*. Belmont CA: Wadsworth Publishing Co., 1988.

Chapter 4
Client Rights

We now turn to examine the issue of duties from the perspective of the client, the issue of client rights.

The idea of "rights" is a recent phenomenon in Western philosophical thought. There is no mention of rights in the works of Plato and Aristotle. The soil from which the idea of "rights" grew is the Renaissance with its emphasis on the autonomy of the individual, as in Pico Della Mirandola (1463–1494) extolling the freedom of human will. Later, Kant (1724–1804) defined "enlightenment" as the ability to use one's own reason without depending on another. The notion of "natural rights" began properly with the works of Thomas Hobbes (1588–1679), John Locke (1632–1704), and Jean Jacques Rousseau (1712–1778). These political philosophers developed the concept of natural rights on the basis of a hypothetical state of nature which exists prior to the formation of governments. In this approach, not only do people have rights, but it is also that they give their consent, which authorizes the formation of governments. These philosophers formed the "social contract" concept in political philosophy.

The ideas of social contract political philosophy came to full bloom in the American Revolution. The idea of "rights" became a cornerstone. In the Declaration of Independence (1776) founders of our nation maintained:

> We hold these truths to be self-evident, that all men are created equal; that they are endowed by their Creator with certain unalienable rights; that among these, are life, liberty, and the pursuit of happiness. That, to secure these rights, governments are instituted among men, deriving their just powers from the consent of the governed.

In this famous paragraph two foundations for rights were put forth. The first is a religious basis which is described in general terms "by their Creator." The second is the conviction that these rights are "self-evident." Regardless of how one grounds "rights" they are "inalienable." Back in Europe, the concept of natural rights also took concrete form in the political arena when in 1789 the authors of the French Declaration of the Rights of Men and Citizens asserted that the rights of "liberty, property, security, and resistance to oppression" are natural, inalienable, and sacred. In 1791 a formal "Bill of Rights" was incorporated into the American Constitution. A significant part of our current political context is made up of a tradition which has a strong emphasis on rights.

The issue of rights was expanded by the early feminist author Mary Wollstonecraft (1759–1797) who launched a critique of the eighteenth century doctrine of the rights of man. In her *Vindication of the Rights of Women* (1792) Wollstonecraft argued that rights are based on rational capacities and that women should hold the same rights as men. The eighteenth century saw the theoretical and practical realization of the concept of rights. A significant part of our current political context is made up of this tradition which has a strong emphasis on rights.

CLASSIFICATION OF RIGHTS

The term "rights," like the term "professional," has been steadily expanding to now include anything of value to human beings. An investigation of rights in marriage and family therapy should not focus on civil and legal rights, but can be done by specifying the nature of and justification for rights that clients possess.

There are three basic categories of rights: the right to life, "freedom" rights, and "positive" rights. There are a variety of words often used to describe human rights: inalienable, indefeasible, core, generic, basic, absolute, fundamental, and universal. Regardless of what words are used, however, traditionally and logically, rights begin with the right to life. This right has generated considerable controversy in our society with the pro-life / pro-choice debate over the abortion issue. The right to life is held to be an intrinsic right: that is, it is valuable in and of itself and one possesses it by virtue of being a human being.

The next category of rights are "freedom" rights, which arise from the right to life. Freedom rights are often described in negative terms—freedom from harm, violence, abuse, unjust treatment, persecution—in general the right not to be interfered with. A positive example of a freedom right is the freedom to practice one's religion. Another example is the right to marry and form a family. Freedom rights are described as prima facie rights (basic rights, but ones that can be overridden in certain circumstances). Basic freedom rights are the rights of autonomy and privacy. The right to privacy is not stated in the Bill of Rights, but Warren and Brandeis argued in their landmark decision (1890) that the right to privacy is implied in the rights contained in the Bill of Rights.[1] Philosophically we need to ask why the right to privacy is important. The right to privacy is crucial to our existence because it underlies our capacity and ability to value, our ability to choose who and what is important to us. A man who cannot choose his friends, has in terms of our Renaissance heritage been robbed of both his freedom and dignity. Likewise, a woman who cannot work in the career of her choice has been similarly robbed. What is at stake here is our ability to act as moral agents making our choices and selecting our values and relationships.

The third category of rights can be described as "positive rights." Examples of positive rights are "well-being rights" described in the United Nations' Universal Declaration of Human Rights. Article 25 describes the right to an adequate standard of living, which includes the right to health care. Article 26 describes the right to an education.[2] Positive rights grew up in the context of social contract political philosophy.

In order to better provide for themselves people formed governments to meet needs which cannot be met individually or in small groups. Such arrangements provide a "contractual" basis for any number of positive rights. Joel Feinberg argues that such rights must have four elements: (1) a content—a specific positive good that is the object of the claim; (2) a holder—someone who possesses the right; (3) an addressee—someone toward whom one's claim is addressed or directed; (4)

---

[1]Werhane, Patricia. "Individual Rights in Business." In *Just Business*, ed. Tom Regan. New York: Random House, 1984, 120.

[2]Feinberg, Joel. "The Nature and Value of Rights." In *The Philosophy of Human Rights*, ed. Morton Winston. Belmont CA: Wadsworth Publishing Co., 1989, 61–74.

a source of validation, i.e., a source of justification for the claim.[3] Foundational political documents and religious creeds are two sources frequently used to justify rights.

With positive or well-being rights, the question to whom are the rights addressed is crucial. Fellow citizens, professional organizations, and institutions have a duty to recognize and fulfill specific rights. For example, the right to an education is addressed to teachers and to schools. The implied addressee of virtually all positive rights is the government. In social contract theory the government either has a responsibility to meet the need generated by the right or at least to guarantee that institutions within the society do so. Thus, governments provide public education with access to all and ensure that citizens have access to private educational institutions.

JUSTIFICATION AND CRITICISM

Though we have seen certain historical sources of rights in the Renaissance and the social contract thinking of the Enlightenment, a more systematic philosophical understanding identifies at least six major approaches to rights and their justification.

The *religious* approach grounds the existence of rights in the sacredness of human life and a belief that this sacredness has a transcendent source. The Judaeo-Christian tradition grounds our sacredness in the Biblical view found in Genesis, that we are created in the image of God. The *conventialist* position maintains that

---

[3]*ibid.*, 67–74.

the moral norms embodied in human rights are in fact social norms formed by the culture. This is also a cultural relativist position which views moral principles as products of the culture. Thus a right to be respected as a person in Japanese culture would include the right to have one's honor respected because of Japanese culture's traditional emphasis on honor. The *prudentialist* theory sees individuals entering into social agreements in which rights are created in order to advance their self-interests. The social contract theories are supported by this approach. The *prudentialist* approach has an egoistic dimension in that people are viewed as selfish and as acting to advance their own basic interests. The *deontological* approach justifies human rights by holding that they are a universal aspect of human nature and are not products of social conventions. The major contribution of this approach is its insistence on the universal application of rights. Kant (1724–1804) developed this view and maintained that a respect for persons is basic to moral philosophy. The United Nations Declaration of Rights is a prime example of this approach. The *utilitarian* theory argues that moral norms embodying human rights represent high priority rules that regulate human behavior and when observed produce the greatest good for the greatest number of people. John Stuart Mill (1806–1873) is a leading proponent of the utilitarian approach. The last theory is the *interdependency* theory, advanced by Henry Shue, who attempts to show that basic rights are necessary for the enjoyment of all other rights.[4] Thus my right to life is crucial because without it my rights to privacy, education, and so on, are meaningless.

---

[4]Shue, Henry. "Security and Subsistence." In *The Philosophy of Human Rights*, ed. Morton Winston. Belmont CA: Wadsworth Publishing Co., 1989, 152–171.

The rights approaches to moral philosophy has not been without its critics. The English utilitarian moral philosopher Jeremy Bentham (1748–1832) argued that rights were "nonsense upon stilts."[5] Another skeptic about human rights is the contemporary moral philosopher Alasdair MacIntyre. MacIntyre maintains that, "There are no human rights, and belief in them is one with belief in witches and unicorns."[6] Human rights, MacIntyre thinks, are moral fictions that may serve useful purposes in moral discourse but do not embody moral truths.

The rights approach to moral philosophy gives rise to two major issues. The first concerns the question of limits on human rights. I have a number of freedom rights which stop when I violate or harm another person and his or her rights and well-being. One of the functions of law in our society has been to define the boundaries between the rights of one person and another. The second related issue that rights theorists have not solved is conflict between rights. Rights theorists tend to enumerate lists of rights but do not address the issue of conflicting rights. What do we do when in a time of scarce economic resources one person's right to health conflicts with another person's right to education? Here we return to the perennial issue of distributive justice.

The issue that all approaches to rights struggle with is the grounding of rights. The existence of rights is, however, ultimately a normative question. Regardless of which theory is used to justify their existence, rights are a normative necessity. That is, they embody moral norms necessary for respecting human beings. Human

---

[5]Winston, Morton, ed., as quoted in *The Philosophy of Human Rights*. Belmont CA: Wadsworth Publishing Co., 1989, 5.

[6]*ibid.*, 29.

rights are, therefore, necessary moral goods. Even if they were, as MacIntyre suggests, moral fictions, they are still necessary to protect a fundamental respect for each person.

THE CORRELATION OF RIGHTS AND DUTIES

Positive rights frequently involve well-being rights which need to be fulfilled by someone else. My right to something involves someone else's duty to fulfill the need implied by my right. In the previous chapter we examined the duties of marriage and family therapists, now we move to correlate rights with duties. This is best done in the social contract context that we have been describing.

We have seen that in our classification of rights that each level is derived from the previous level. We began with the basic right to life. This right implies that the therapist has a duty to respect the right to life of clients as well as of all human beings. Thus if a client is threatening harm to someone else, the therapist has a duty to protect (warn) that person because each person has this same fundamental right to life.

At this point the duties we have examined in the previous chapter need to be viewed from the clients' perspective in terms of the "rights" that clients hold.

The first of Ross's duties is *reparation*. Therapists perform this duty not because they are therapists but because they are human beings. If in the process of therapy a client is harmed by a mistake or something that I say, I have a duty to repair that harms as much as I am able. This involves owning the mistake and when appropriate apologizing to the client. The corresponding right from the client's perspective is the right to be respected.

The second duty is that of *fidelity*. I have a duty to honor my promises and commitments. This duty is initially expressed in the contracting phase of therapy. Therapists have a particular responsibility to honor the contract that they have agreed to unless circumstances change dramatically and it is impossible to keep fidelity with the contract. Clients have a right to be treated with trust which is an essential ingredient in the concept of respect for persons.

Ross's third duty is that of *gratitude*. William May points out that professionals owe a debt to society because essential parts of their training takes place in colleges and universities which are supported by our society. This duty can be expressed by as far as one is able to see clients at low fees or no fees at all. In this sense clients have a right to be helped regardless of economic circumstances. In turn, clients, once they are doing better economically, likewise have a duty of gratitude, to help others receive the therapy they need.

The fourth duty is *beneficence*. This duty is part of our reason for being marriage and family therapists. Every time we meet with our clients we are expressing our commitment to help others. Viewed from the client's perspective, clients have a right to therapeutic help. As I have pointed out in the first chapter, this should not be limited to middle and upper class clients.

Ross's fifth duty is that of *non-harm*. In medical ethics the first responsibility of the physician is *primum non nocere*, to do no harm. This fifth duty is the reverse side of the duty of beneficence. Our clients have a right not to be harmed. This includes being warned that the process they are entering may produce harmful consequences. The prime example is marriage counseling which initially attempts to help both partners clarify if they want to continue the relationship. Here the therapist cannot rescue people from the harmful (or helpful) consequences of separation and divorce. The therapist can and should explain the risk involved by engaging in the process.

The sixth duty is that of *justice*. Therapists have a duty to treat people fairly. This applies especially to their clients since clients, because of their needs, have a greater degree of vulnerability. Clients have a right to just treatment in the development of their therapeutic contracts. Therapists are in the business of working for a balance of power that can best be described as justice.

Ross's last duty is that of *self-improvement*. We have seen how this involves a process of continuing education for the family therapist. Our field is in a constant process of growth and development. Family therapists have a duty to be a part of this development. Our clients have a right to the best quality of marriage and family therapy that we are able to provide. Part of being a professional involves a commitment to excellence in what we do. We need to bring that commitment into everything we do in our profession.

Karen Lebacqz added two duties to those enumerated by Ross. For Lebacqz, professionals have a duty to respect the autonomy of their clients. The AAMFT Code of Ethics recognizes this duty in section 1:4 of the code: "Therapists clearly advise a client that a decision on marital status is the responsibility of the client." Clients have a right to have their autonomy respected and this involves recognizing that the decisions about their marriages and families belong to them. Therapists need to be careful that we do not even in subtle ways diminish our client's autonomy.

The final duty, described by Lebacqz, is the duty to *tell the truth*. I do not view the truth as a singular objective entity that I deliver to the client, but rather that I help clients by means of my objectivity and that I help them look at their lives from different perspectives. In this sense the duty of telling the truth is expanded for family therapists to evoking possibilities. We work to help our clients get unstuck. Clients have a right to the truths about their lives and relationships. To deceive a client would be to undermine the fiduciary nature of the therapeutic relationship.

Professional associations in the health-related field have begun to look at ethical issues from the perspective of the rights of clients.

The National Board of Certified Counselors has affirmed the following ten rights of clients:[7]

1. The right to be informed of the qualifications and experience of the counselor.

2. The right to an explanation of the services offered; the therapist's time commitment; and fees and billing policies prior to the receipt of services.

3. The right to be informed of the counselor's limitations of practice to specific areas of expertise and age groups.

4. The right to ask questions about counseling techniques and to be informed of progress.

5. The right to participation in setting goals and the evaluation of progress in reaching them.

---

[7]*Counseling Services: Consumer Rights and Responsibilities.* The National Board of Certified Counselors, Alexandria, VA, 1990.

6. The right to know how to contact the counselor in an emergency.

7. The right to request a second opinion or a referral for a second opinion.

8. The right to request copies of records and reports to be used by other professionals.

9. The right to receive a copy of the code of ethics to which the counselor adheres.

10. The right to contact appropriate professional organizations if the client has doubts or complaints relative to the counselor's conduct.

These rights were formed in the context of individual therapy and assume one therapist, one client. Marriage and family therapy treats relationships and conceptualizes problems primarily in interpersonal terms. Therefore, marriage and family therapy takes place in a context that has significant differences from that of individual therapy. Clients have a number of additional rights in marriage and family therapy.

11. Clients have a right to refuse treatment. Since this is traditionally an individual right, it poses dilemmas for family therapy which treats relationships.

Case
A couple comes in for family therapy requesting help in dealing with their three children. In the initial sessions the father's resistance to therapy increases in spite of the therapist's attempts to connect with him. The wife comes to the sixth session by herself and reports that her husband does not want to continue in therapy. The wife needs support at this point to work with the rest of the family, but this could widen the gulf between the husband and his family. The therapist is caught between respecting the husband's choice and the needs of the rest of the family. The therapist is also aware of a responsibility to not make things worse.

12. Clients have a right to know about the therapist's theories, values, and beliefs. This includes the right to diagnostic and assessment information.

Case

A family therapist works primarily from a Bowen family of origin model with additional techniques from the Milan approach. These are described in a six page handout which contains the therapist's beliefs about couples, families and the nature of therapy. Clients are given this handout during the first session. In addition, after four sessions the therapist shares diagnostic and assessment information with the clients and sets treatment goals with the clients.

13. Clients have a right to be respected and to be seen as unique. This includes having one's ethnic and religious traditions respected. Family therapists differ in terms of how they view the role of ethnicity in families. Some therapists see ethnicity as a prime factor that makes a great deal of difference in terms of how families function. Others maintain that family issues, like enmeshment, for example, are the same regardless of what cultural envelope they come in.

Case

A second generation Greek-American couple make an appointment for marital therapy. The couple have a severely conflicted relationship. The therapist, without any experience or knowledge of Greek culture, shows respect for this dimension by inquiring how Greek culture views staying together no matter how troubled the couple is about their relationship. At appropriate times in the therapy, the therapist inquires as to how the Greek culture views a particular issue.

14. Clients have rights in family therapy to have decisions about relationships left with them. As previously stated, clients have a right to have their autonomy respected. The therapist is responsible for bringing objectivity and clarity to the process, but not in making or unduly influencing decisions. Therapists have a duty to warn of possible harmful (and beneficial) consequences of choices.

Case

An individual woman calls and makes an appointment for herself. In the initial interview the client clearly states that she wants marital therapy. The therapist explains the difference between individual and marital therapy. Since the woman has not made a decision to end the relationship, the therapist explains that marital therapy would be the most appropriate type of therapy for examining their relationship. The therapist also explains that to set up individual therapy is to set up an empathetic and "loving" relationship between them which could easily make the alienation in the marriage worse.

15. Clients have rights to a collaborative and respectful therapeutic process. Family

therapy is not something done to people but rather a process in which they are

involved—it is a collaborative effort. Clients have a right not to be manipulated,

i.e., be treated as an end in oneself and not as a means to an end.

Case
A family therapist with fifteen years experience begins attending a weekly peer review group with five colleagues. In spite of his experience, the therapist learns a great deal from his colleagues. He adopts the same attitude with his clients and begins to learn from them. There is an isomorphism here between his posture as learner with his colleagues as well as with his clients.

A final issue emerges from our analysis and correlation of rights and duties,

based upon Article 25 of the United Nations Declaration of Rights (the right to

health care). I maintain that people have a right to a full range of health care

services. This includes the right to marriage and family therapy. It is clearly beyond

the resources of AAMFT to provide marriage and family therapy on a national

scale. AAMFT has been working on influencing public policy in the area of

providing services. This involves us in the myriad of political and economic issues

involved in the formation of a national health care system.

In this chapter I have examined the types, history, and justification of rights.

This has enabled us to begin to look at ethical issues in family therapy from the

perspectives of our clients. Finally, I have correlated rights with their

corresponding duties.

Chapter 5
Developmental Moral Theory

INTRODUCTION

Having examined the duties of therapists and the rights of clients from the perspective of moral philosophy, it is only fitting that we complement such an analysis with empirical information about how human beings and their families develop morally. The major studies to date are those of Robert Coles, the social learning theorist, and Lawrence Kohlberg and Carol Gilligan.

Robert Coles describes his approach to moral development as "documentary child psychiatry." Coles won a Pulitzer Prize for his five volume "Children of Crisis" series. He combines his own experience with the insights of literature to understand the moral lives of children.[1]

Coles' work was inspired by the moral and spiritual sensitivity of a young black girl, Ruby Bridges, in the South in the early days of the civil rights movement. Ruby was the only black girl in a newly integrated elementary school. Each day she was walked to school by a group of federal marshals who were there to protect her from the angry mob. One day Ruby stopped midway on her walk to school. She appeared to be saying a few words, then resumed her walk to school. Coles was concerned about her stopping since this gave her greater exposure to the mob. Coles asked Ruby why she had stopped. Ruby explained that every morning

---

[1]Lageman, August. "The Moral Lives of Children: The Thought of Robert Coles." *Journal of Religion and Health* 29 (1990): 303–307.

she said her prayers before leaving for school, and on that particular day she had forgotten to say her prayers. Ruby remembered on her way to school and that is why she stopped to pray. Coles asked her how she felt about the angry mob. Ruby replied that she was praying for these people. Ruby then turned the table on Coles, asking him a question: Don't you think these people need praying for?

Robert Coles' work is built upon Gordon Allport's distinction between character and personality. For Coles human beings have a moral center which he describes as character. This distinction stands in sharp contrast to modern psychology, which has for the most part focused on the human personality. Coles is critical of psychology's extensive investigations into character disorders (psychopathic and sociopathic disorders) without first having a clear concept of what constitutes a healthy character. Here Coles builds on Abraham Maslow's work on understanding healthy human beings. For our purposes one contribution of Coles stands out, his view that *the moral purpose of the family is to develop character*. Thus families are where we learn values and how to treat other people. We literally learn what is important in life: thus the foundations of our characters are built. We learn about honesty, fairness, and consideration. Since families are in the business of developing character, family therapists are responsible for assisting in this process. In order to clarify this responsibility, we need to learn more about moral development.

SOCIAL LEARNING THEORIES

Social learning theory holds that moral formation consists in the acquisition of norms of behavior which are taken in from one's immediate external environment. For most children the home and the school are the immediate environments. Through a process of learning, the individual begins to observe rules and norms on the basis of rewards and punishments. The process is complete only when individuals have taken on the rules as their own in the process of internalization. This approach can be described as "prosocial" in that relevant rules are set by society and mediated to the individual by parents, teachers, and other social agents in the environment.

The social learning theory is an empiricist-based approach begun by B. F. Skinner and H. J. Eysenck. It places major emphasis on forms of conditioning (in contrast to cognitive approaches which we will examine later in this chapter). H. J. Eysenck describes the developed nature of conscience:

> Our contention will be that conscience is simply conditioned reflex and that it originates in the same ways as phobic and neurotic responses...in other words when the child is going to carry out one of the many activities which have been prohibited and punished in the past (the slap, the moral shaming, or whatever the punishment may be), then the conditioned automatic response would immediately occur and produce a strong deterrent, being as it were, unpleasant in itself.[2]

Eysenck thus attempts to explain how external rules are "internalized" by a person so as to give rise to moral (socially approved) behavior. Eysenck's idea of conscience is conditioned anxiety, affected primarily through punishment. Thus conscience is basically a conditioned reflex. The social learning theory has roots in

---

[2]Eysenck, H. J. *Fact and Fiction in Psychology*. Harmondsworth: Penguin Books, 1965, 260.

seventeenth century philosophy. John Locke (1632–1704), the English empiricist philosopher, developed his epistemology (theory of knowledge) upon the concept of the human mind as a tabula rosa, a blank tablet upon which experience writes.

Many social learning theorists have expressed dissatisfaction with the narrow behaviorist account of moral learning. A second concept of conscience as cognitive and evaluative has emerged. In this approach cognitive and evaluative considerations are considered in relation to moral judgment and conduct, and there is an attempt to see the person as a moral agent (not simply the locus when genetic and environmental conditions come together) who self-regulates in connection with internalized moral values. Justin Aronfreed, in his book *Conduct and Conscience*, attempts to develop a fuller version of the social learning theory which deals with the cognitive and affective dimensions of values and morals.[3]

COGNITIVE DEVELOPMENTAL THEORY

In contrast to the empirical basis of the social learning approach, cognitive theorists have focused on the role of cognitive considerations in the development of the moral dimension of human beings. Lawrence Kohlberg is the leading exponent of the cognitive approach. Kohlberg uses the psychological theories of Erik Erikson and Jean Piaget to chart the moral dimension of human development.[4] Kohlberg's "stages" are the first systematic attempt to integrate developmental psychology with moral philosophy. For Kohlberg, moral development begins in the first years of a

---

[3]Aronfreed, Justin. *Conduct and Conscience*. New York: Academic Press, 1968.

[4]Kohlberg, Lawrence. *Essays on Moral Development*. Vol. I. San Francisco: Harper and Row, 1984.

child's life with stages one and two together described as "preconventional." Stages three and four are the stages of childhood and adolescence that introduce the young to the "conventions" of the social order. Finally, in adult development, there is the opportunity to develop principles and apply them universally (post-conventional). Many people stay in stages three and four and do not move to the post-conventional stages. Kohlberg does not view his stages as automatic and recognizes that people can regress to operate at an earlier stage of development. We can better understand our own moral dilemmas as family therapists as well as the moral dilemmas that our clients face by understanding the stages of moral development.

1. In stage one, punishment and obedience, a small child first learns what is right and wrong by means of the "power" that parents and other adults have over the child. This is an egocentric stage of moral development. Often our adult clients are operating at this stage of moral development and are unaware of how egocentric their ways of relating are. Therapists also operate at this stage. A therapist refuses to accept a gift from a client because the agency she works for has a policy which prohibits the acceptance of gifts.

2. In the second stage, that of *individual instrumental purpose and exchange*, a pre-school child feels that what is right is what satisfies his own needs (I took her toy because I needed it). What is right is related to rules insofar as they serve my own immediate interests. I recognize the needs of others only because by doing so they, in turn, are willing to help me advance my own interests. This is the concrete individualistic point of view.

We see the survival of this stage in the therapist who refers certain types of clients to another clinician who specializes in treating those clients but with the understanding that the other clinician will refer appropriate clients in return. This is an exchange predicated on the therapist meeting his own needs.

CONVENTIONAL LEVEL

3. The next stage is of *mutual interpersonal expectations, relationship, and conformity*. Both at home and in school the child is socialized and learns that it is good to please and help others. What is right and good is related to the expectations of others. Emphasis is on concern for others and relating with trust, loyalty, respect, and gratitude. At this stage the child develops as having shared feelings and agreements with others. With this stage a crucial step has occurred—the leap from self to others in moral development.

In our work as therapists we operate at this level. The roles of therapist and client are defined and mutually understood. The therapeutic exchange is predicated on a mutuality built upon meeting one another's needs. In light of the egocentricity of the first two stages, family therapists need to be relating to clients at this stage of moral development. This should be viewed as a minimal level for our work with couples and families.

4. The fourth stage is that of *social system and conscience*. The child learns that he or she has a duty to obey the rules of the school. What is right is formed by one's duties to uphold the social order and to maintain the welfare of the society,

group, or institution. One has a duty to keep the social system going and one feels an obligation to do this, and, thus, acts out of a sense of conscience.

Duty to one's professional organization arise at this stage of moral development.

POST-CONVENTIONAL OR PRINCIPLED LEVEL

5. The fifth stage is of *social contract or utility and individual rights*. In this stage a person is concerned with upholding the basic rights, values, and contracts of society. The individual recognizes the principles embedded in the social order and has moved beyond the conformity of the previous stage. This is the stage of "principled" ethical thinking. In this stage of moral development a person would break a "law" (civil disobedience) if it violated a moral principle. A person can now recognize the possibility and necessity of changing the social contract. At this stage the value of impartiality is recognized in moral deliberations. The rights and well-being of all are recognized in this stage. Emphasis is now put on the principle of utility—the greatest good for the greatest number of people—which forms the basis of a concept of justice.

Case
A family is in therapy for problems with two teenage children. In one of the sessions in which the therapist is working with the parents, the father comes in agitated. He is an engineer and has discovered a major safety flaw in the farm equipment that his company makes. His boss is pressuring him to keep quiet because the flaw would be too expensive to fix. The issue is a classic one of "whistleblowing." Public safety is a prime concern. The threat of a loss of a job, economic hardship on the family, and difficulties in obtaining future employment are all important considerations.

6. The last stage is *universal ethical principles*. The individual has chosen certain ethical principles in the previous stage and is now able to transcend race, ethnic,

and class barriers, and apply his or her ethical principles to all human beings. The person recognizes the equality of human rights and respect for the dignity of human beings as individual persons. In this stage a person is able to universalize his or her ethical principles.

This stage is particularly important for marriage and family therapists. Because of the healing—the therapeutic nature of what we do—we need to appreciate and understand the rich diversity of the human community. At the same time we need to commit ourselves to a fundamental ethical principle of respect for persons. This respect is "recognition respect" that is a moral attitude due all people including oneself, simply because we are all human beings.[5] This is different from "appraisal respect" which involves respect because of characteristics, ability, achievement, or some form of accomplishment.

Kohlberg's six stages revolve around three levels of ethical concern. Initially, a person is concerned with his or her own immediate interests and needs with regard to external rewards and punishments (pre-conventional). At the second level, an individual defines right as conforming to the expectations of good behavior of the larger society or some significant reference group (conventional). Finally, there is the level of principles, in which an individual sees beyond the norms, laws, and authority of groups (post-conventional).

---

[5]Darwall, Stephen. "Two Kinds of Respect." *Ethics* 88 (1977).

ASSESSMENT AND CRITICISMS OF KOHLBERG

Kohlberg has provided us with the first map of moral development from infancy to adulthood. It is not, however, without its problems.

Stage five of Kohlberg's model is founded on social contract philosophy and contains a concept of justice associated with utilitarian moral theory. Stage six, which is for Kohlberg the epitome of moral development (with its emphasis on universality) contains a deontological approach historically associated with Kant. Thus there is a distinct difference between the directions of stages five and six.

John Rawls clearly describes the differences between the empiricist/utilitarian traditions and rational/deontological approach:

> ...right conduct is conduct generally beneficial to others and to society (as defined by the principle of utility) for the doing of which we commonly lack an effective motive, whereas wrong conduct is behaviour generally injurious to others and to society and for the doing of which we often have a sufficient motive. Society must somehow make good these defects. This is achieved by the approbation and disapprobation of parents and others in authority, who when necessary use rewards and punishments ranging from bestowal and withdrawal of affection to the administration of pleasures and pains. Eventually by various psychological processes we acquire a desire to do what is right and an aversion to doing what is wrong.

In the rationalist tradition of moral learning, he continues:

> ...moral learning is not so much a matter of supplying missing motives as one of the free development of our innate intellectual and emotional capacities according to their natural bent. Once the powers of understanding mature, and persons come to recognize their place in society and are able to take the standpoint of others, they appreciate the mutual benefits of establishing fair terms of social cooperation. We have a natural sympathy with other persons and an innate susceptibility to the pleasure of fellow-feeling and self-mastery, and these provide the affective basis for our moral sentiments once we have a clear grasp of our relations to our associates from an appropriately general perspective.[6]

---

[6]Rawls, John. *A Theory of Justice*. London: Oxford University Press, 1972, 458–460.

There is a tension between these two divergent strands in Kohlberg's model. Kohlberg's theory resolves this tension in favor of Kant's universalist approach. Ironically, at the same time, Kohlberg's developmental stages provide us with a basis for criticizing Kant's assumption that we are all moral and rational adults. This is important for family therapists because we would miss significant moral issues in our work with clients if we were to make Kant's assumption.

A problem with Kohlberg's stages concerns his claim to have developed a model which is culturally universal. Subsequent empirical studies by Ian Vine and Carol Edwards have shown that there is little unambiguous evidence to support stages five and six in non-Western cultures.[7]

Kohlberg's major flaw was his use of only male subjects for his empirical studies. Kohlberg's research was begun in the 1950s and involved a cross-sectional study of the ways in which children and adolescents responded to a range of hypothetical dilemmas. This was followed by a major longitudinal study of some 58 subjects from the original group and a variety of cross-sectional studies in different cultures. Carol Gilligan, in *A Different Voice*, examines the male bias in Kohlberg's research.The ethic of justice emphasizes autonomy, individual rights, equality, and the rational resolution of conflict that casts a shadow back over the earlier stages and shows ethical principles which mark points in the (male) individual's quest for identity, independence, separation, and autonomy. This view

---

[7]Vine, Ian. "Moral Maturity in Socio-Cultural Perspective: Are Kohlberg's Stages Universal?" In *Lawrence Kohlberg, Consensus and Controversy*, ed. S. Modgil and C. Modgil. 431–450. Lewes U.K.: Falmer Press, 1985. Edwards, C. P. "Cross-Cultural Research on Kohlberg's Stages: The Basis for Consensus." In *Lawrence Kohlberg, Consensus and Controversy*, ed. S. Modgil and C. Modgil. 419–430. Lewes, U. K.: Falmer Press, 1985.

is founded on a view of human beings as separate and objective in relation to others.[8]

Gilligan accepts Kohlberg's stages as valid for male moral development. In what is now called the twin paths doctrine, Gilligan posits an ethic of care (instead of an ethic of justice) which conceptualizes maturity in a different way. The ethic of care emphasizes connectedness in relationship to others: attachment, mutuality, and response to others. The central insight of the ethic of care is that self and others are interdependent. Gilligan puts particular weight on her own inquiries in responses to concrete moral dilemmas. Gilligan ends up with a type of casuistry (the idea that moral principles emerge from cases—instead of the approach which works in the other direction from theory to cases). Gilligan's approach is thus a form of contextual relativism. Gilligan's work has brought the issue of sexual differences in moral development to the forefront of developmental research. Her ethic of care, which takes the feminine perspective into account, regards individuals as connected in relations to others, and involved in responsive and caring ways, a view more congruent with family system approaches (which treat the relationships and not individuals). It is important to apply these theories of moral development to our work with clients.

Case
A couple is in therapy with their children (girl sixteen, boy thirteen). The presenting problem was discipline with both children. The daughter has been cutting classes in school. The son has recently been put on probation because he was caught cheating on an exam. The father mentions in passing the fringe benefits he gets from his job by "taking" office supplies. You become aware that the mother has been working a part time job and getting paid under the table.

---

[8]Gilligan, Carol. *In A Different Voice*. Cambridge MA: Harvard University Press, 1982.

Both parents are modeling cheating to their children and are unwittingly

contributing to their childrens' problems. The therapeutic task, then, is, without

being moralistic and judgmental, to help the parents understand how their modeling

contributes to their childrens' problems and to help all concerned grow toward a

higher level of moral development. This case, in a negative way, illustrates Robert

Coles' idea that families develop character.

Case
A couple comes in for therapy with their three children (girl eleven, boy
nine, girl six). The boy and youngest girl are having behavior problems in
school and they fight constantly at home. The oldest daughter is withdrawn
and depressed. As the therapist begins to work with the parents, both
shame their children and do not know how to nurture their childrens' self-
esteem.

In the case both the emotional and moral development of the children is being

crippled. If this shame-based approach had gone unchecked it would produce

children with rigid and legalistic moral ideation designed to help them avoid being

shamed. Research needs to be done into the effects of shaming on moral

development.

Case
A father calls in for therapy. He comes in to the initial appointment by
himself. The father is very angry about his inability to control his fourteen
year old son. The father is rigid in his discipline of his son. The rest of the
family (the mother and a sixteen year old daughter) refuse to come in for
therapy claiming the problem is between the two of them.

The therapeutic task is to help the father get in touch with his underdeveloped

nurturing side and in a sense introduce the "feminine side" into their relationship.

The therapist introduces a new set of values for their relationship. Family therapy

thus becomes, at least in part, an exercise in both the clarification and teaching of

values.

DEVELOPMENTAL MORAL THEORY AND ORGANIZATION

Developmental moral theory can be applied to organizations that go through stages of development both organizationally and morally. The following six stages provide a vehicle for assessing the moral climate in an organization.

Stage One: Social Darwinism

At this stage fear of extinction and the urgency of financial survival form the moral climate. Any means which facilitates survival is acceptable. Organizations which are about to collapse and die often revert to this stage. Anything goes and the organization is preoccupied with the goal of survival.

Stage Two: Machiavellian

At this level organizational growth dominates the corporate culture. Power and manipulation are valued because they help the organization succeed. The end justifies the means. New organizations often experience this stage. Power is the primary value in the organization. Moral questions or issues are not raised.

Stage Three: Popular Conformity

At this stage the organization has developed standard operating procedures. Peer pressure helps to reinforce adherence to the norms of the organization. The organization works by consensus. Nonprofit organizations frequently operate in this stage. The goal is to make everyone happy and productive.

Stage Four: Allegiance to Authority

At this level the organization has developed to a greater degree of complexity. Hierarchy is recognized as important. Right and wrong is determined by those in authority. Structure is valued and loyalty is a prime virtue. Military and paramilitary organizations, such as police departments, frequently function at this stage.

Stage Five: Democratic Participation

At this level, participation in the decision-making process is central to the organization's life. The majority rules. Popular forms of utilitarianism (the greater good for the greatest number) make up the moral atmosphere of the organization. Nonprofit organizations that provide marriage and family therapy instinctively want to operate at this stage. The tension arises when the organization is of sufficient size and complexity as to require a hierarchical structure for the organization to function. If the organization stage stays at this level it will get bogged down in "process" because the organization norm is that everyone has to agree.

Stage Six: Organizational Integrity

At this stage, care, respect for the individual, and justice are core values. The tension between individuals and the organization is openly acknowledged. People struggle to bring the organization into line with their own moral visions. The moral dimension of organizational life is openly acknowledged and discussed.

Not only do individuals and organizations develop morally, but families are the primary context in which we develop morally.

THE INTERGENERATIONAL DIMENSION

Ivan Boszormenyi-Nagy has developed a "contextual" approach to families which considers families not just in the here and now but throughout the generations of a family's life.

For Boszormenyi-Nagy there are four dimensions to families. The first is the dimension of external fact, which is the historical life of the family. This dimension includes migrations, income level, illnesses and deaths, political, economic, and social conditions throughout the family's life. A family's unique history and significant family events can be understood in part by a genogram (an intergenerational map) of the family. The second dimension is that of the psychological, which is the level of the emotional life of the family. This level involves the emotional climate and atmosphere of the family. What does it feel like to be a part of this family? The psychological dimension includes the intrapsychic health and illnesses of each member. The next level is the transactional which consists of the relational and interactive processes of the family. How have the members related to one another? How have the children been raised? In this family, how have women treated men and vice versa? For Boszormenyi-Nagy, the final dimension is that of the ethical. How has this family dealt with the moral issues that family life inevitably raises?

Ivan Boszormenyi-Nagy maintains that issues of "fairness" and "trust" are present in all relationships. He has developed concepts of a "ledger" (how the investment of people in one another is balanced overtime) and "legacy" (which involves the positive and negative inheritances which are passed down through the generations). Nagy develops other concepts (exploitation, exoneration, entitlement, and split loyalty) which further map the moral dimension of the intergenerational phenomenon which we call a family.

Boszormenyi-Nagy, with his intergenerational model of families, clearly demonstrates that the moral life of the family has a strong intergenerational component. This gives us yet another perspective as we examine the moral dimensions of marriage and family therapy. It also forces us to re-examine some of the moral theory that has already been applied. Kant, with his insistence on impartiality and universality, has provided us with one of the classic ethical theories. Barbara Herman, in "Agency, Attachment, and Difference," points out that Kant's approach assumes that people are moral equals.[9] Family relationships, specifically between parents and children, are inherently unequal. There is a deep bond of mutual attachment between parent and child, and, hopefully, this is a relationship of trust; but it is clearly trust between unequals. Herman points out that:

> ...relationships of attachment pose a serious problem for Kantian ethics if attachment is a source of distinctive moral claims that impartiality disallows, or if the features of persons that support and express attachment are devalued by its conception of moral agency.[10]

Boszormenyi-Nagy's system, while providing a map of intergenerational moral issues, is difficult to use in that his concepts and four levels are interrelated. This internal difficulty prevents many family therapists from using relevant parts of his system.

CONCLUSION

This chapter began with Robert Coles' idea that the moral purpose of the family is to develop character. Social learning and cognitive developmental approaches to moral development have been examined. With the help of Ivan Boszormenyi-Nagy the moral dimension of families across generations has been studied. Family therapists need to know about moral development and include it as an integral part of their work.

---

[9]Herman, Barbara. "Agency, Attachment, and Difference." *Ethics* 101 (1991).

[10]*ibid.*, 42.

Moral development applies not only to clients but equally to family therapists. Are we content to remain on a conventional level adhering to the AAMFT Code of Ethics, or do we aspire to post-conventional standards embodied in Kohlberg's ethic of justice and Gilligan's ethic of care?

Family therapists have a responsibility to address the moral dimensions of family life in their work with their clients. Family therapists have an opportunity to unite quite different traditions in moral philosophy—the emphasis on emotions exemplified by David Hume (1711–1776) and the rationalist tradition represented by Immanuel Kant (1724–1804). Reason and emotion both occupy significant places in our moral lives. Family therapists are in a unique position to integrate reason and emotion as we address our own moral lives as well as the moral lives of the families with whom we work.[11]

---

[11] Solomon, Robert. *A Passion for Justice: Emotions and the Origins of the Social Contract.* New York: Addison Wesley, 1990.

Chapter 6
Character—Virtue Based Ethics

We have just finished examining the major approaches to moral development. Implied in research and theorizing about moral development is a teleological question: What is the goal of the developmental journey? In terms of family therapists—what are the ingredients of a "good" therapist.

AN INTRODUCTION TO VIRTUE-BASED ETHICS

In the history of Western ethical theory there has been an ongoing debate about the starting point for ethical theory. For some theorists the fundamental question is, "What should I do?" In other words, what types of behaviors are appropriate? Duty-based (deontological) approaches to ethics begin with duties but move in a behavioral direction. Utilitarian approaches move in a behavioral direction and focus on consequences as the primary factor in making moral judgments. For marriage and family therapists, how we behave with our clients is of primary importance. But the ways in which we relate do not comprise the whole of the ethical arena.

For Aristotle the fundamental question is, "How should human beings live?" Oversimplifying the richness and complexity of Aristotle's thought, his answer is whatever leads to excellence ("areté"-the Greek term for virtue). This broader focus enables us, while not excluding behaviors and consequences, to focus on reflecting on moral identity and values. To whom am I morally speaking? We are now able to move to inquire about the "person" of the therapist.

In the previous chapter I examined moral development individually and organizationally. It is important to examine this issue from an historical perspective. Christie W. Kiefer, in her book *The Mantle of Maturity: A History of Ideas About Character Development*, examines the history of how we have looked at character development.[1] The medieval epitome of maturity is the concept of the hero. The medieval hero (usually male) is an explorer and adventurer who conquers the evil opposing forces (the dragons). Kiefer maintains that in the late eighteenth and early nineteenth centuries a shift occurred from this medieval ideal of heroism to a new ideal of maturity. This new concept of maturity was further defined in terms of the new work ethic as success. The mature person is successful in work and in personal relationships. It was in this context that Freud did his epoch-making work. For Freud the mature person is able to control sexual and aggressive drives. Freud's method of psychoanalysis was an attempt to help the individual recover from the intrapsychic price that was paid in the taming of the sexual and aggressive drives.

In the twentieth century we have moved to further redefine maturity as mental health (obviously continuing our medical and psychiatric heritages). It makes more sense to operate from a four dimensional model of health. In addition to the obvious dimension of physical health, we need emotional, relational, and moral dimensions. Mature persons have a high degree of emotional health. They are in touch with their emotions and are free from crippling intrapsychic conflicts. They have a sense of self-esteem. These individuals are capable of meeting their needs in mutually loving

---

[1]Kiefer, Christie W. *The Mantle of Maturity: A History of Ideas About Character Development*. Albany: State University of New York Press, 1988.

and affirming relationships. These relationships are relatively free from destructive interpersonal conflicts. Finally, mature persons have an awareness of the moral dimension and have moral beliefs and principles by which they live. These individuals have a moral strength which we define as "character." People with these last three dimensions of health can be said to be "mature."

Long ago Aristotle investigated the concept of character by means of examination of virtue. For Aristotle, the basic question is, "What is the good life?" In his *Nichomachean Ethics*, Aristotle defined the "good" as "eudaimonia" or happiness. For Aristotle, happiness is living the life of a rational being who has defined the "good" in terms of the virtues by which one lives. Virtue, according to Aristotle, can be defined as the golden mean between excess and defect. One errs, morally speaking, by too much or too little. Aristotle also distinguishes between two kinds of virtues: the objective and the practical. Objective virtues, such as rigorousness and objectivity, are essential to cognitive thought and practical virtues, such as honesty, compassion, and temperance; are essential to a good life in society. Virtues are dispositions or habits which we learn and subsequently practice in daily life. The virtues that we practice make up the type of character that we develop. They determine the kind of person we will be and ultimately have a profound effect on the quality of life we will lead. For Aristotle, both objective and practical virtues can be developed by rational processes and are intrinsically good.

Alasdair MacIntyre, in *After Virtue,* builds on Aristotle and expands our understanding of virtue. MacIntyre argues that the various concepts of virtue advanced throughout history can be understood within a single, complex core concept that involves three dimensions. First, a virtue is an excellence exhibited within a social context. It cannot be practiced in isolation. Second, virtues sustain

us in a lifetime quest to define the good by which all other goods are properly

understood. Virtues lead us to examine a basic philosophical question: What is the

meaning and purpose of life? Finally, virtues contribute to the preservation of those

historical traditions with which both practices and the narrative history of individual

quests for the good are naturally embedded. MacIntyre reasons that,

> A practice involves standards of excellence and obedience to rules as well as
> the achievement of goods. To enter into a practice is to accept the authority
> of those standards and the inadequacy of my own performance as judged by
> them. It is to subject my own attitudes, choices, preferences, and tastes to
> the standards which currently and partially define the practice. Practices of
> course, as I have noticed, have a history: games, science, and art all have
> histories. Thus the standards are not themselves immune from criticism, but
> nonetheless, we cannot be initiated into a practice without accepting the
> authority of the best standards realized so far.[2]

MacIntyre's approach thus clearly locates an examination of virtues in

professional life in both social and historical contexts. In this sense a profession is a

community of practice within these contexts. For our purposes, the key notion here

is initiation into the standards of a community of practice.

It is within the community of practice that virtues need to be identified and

defined. Virtues are the *internal goods* (as opposed to external goods such as fame,

fortune, recognition, and power) which make the core of values at the heart of the

practice of marriage and family therapy. MacIntyre's expansion of the immediate

context of virtues as the community of practice helps us to overcome the

individualism so characteristic of contemporary American culture.

---

[2]MacIntyre, Alasdair. *After Virtue.* South Bend: Notre Dame University Press, 1981.

A FIDUCIARY MODEL

Through the 1950s the prevalent model of ethics in American society was a paternalistic one which viewed the decision making as the professional's responsibility. In medical ethics the physician knew what was best for the patient and was expected to act accordingly. Our society has moved steadily away from paternalism to more collaborative models of professional ethics. This movement is appropriate because the earlier paternalistic approach contained a major ethical flaw—it took the decision making away from the client and his or her family. Thus paternalistic approaches failed to adequately respect the client and his or her rights.

Contemporary marriage and family therapy needs a model of professional ethics which avoids the hierarchy of previous paternalistic approaches. Michael Bayles proposes a fiduciary model in which the professional's knowledge and expertise are crucial, but which at the same time preserves the client's responsibility for decision making.[3] This model emphasizes the therapist's obligation to be worthy of the client's trust. Without trust the possibility of a therapeutic relationship crumbles. Sissela Bok points out that, "Whatever matters to human beings, trust is the atmosphere in which it thrives."[4] Bayles describes a number of virtues which he thinks are essential for the professional.

Five of Bayles' virtues relate specifically to the practice of marriage and family therapy. The first virtue is honesty. The family therapist is honest with his or

---

[3]Bayles, Michael. "Trust and the Professional-Client Relationship." In *Professional Ideals*, ed. Albert Flores. Belmont CA: Wadsworth Publishing Co., 1988, 66–79.

[4]Bok, Sissela. *Lying: Moral Choice in Public and Private Life*. New York: Random House, 1978, 31.

her transactions with clients. The therapist is in a sense the client's agent and avoids dishonesty because it interferes with a trustful relationship. Honesty is critical in the contractual aspects of the therapeutic relationship. In financial dealings with clients, the therapist should ask: "What would I want to occur if I were in the client's financial position?" Honesty in the therapeutic process can easily become complicated. A therapist who honestly describes his or her negative feelings to a client could easily harm the relationship and the client's self-esteem. The context for honesty is the well-being of the client. The therapist is a person of integrity. Erik Erikson, in his monumental study of the life cycle, concluded that the final stage of human development was that of integrity. The therapist's own integrity and commitment to be appropriately honest with clients are essential ingredients in the therapeutic process.

The second virtue is competence. Bayles argues that this is an essential virtue for any profession. Competence, in Aristotelian terms, is a combination of an intellectual and a practical virtue. The family therapist has a thorough knowledge of marriage and family theory. At the same time, the therapist is able to practice the therapeutic skills with clients. This involves translating various aspects of theory into one's interacting with clients. The family therapist is involved in a continuing interaction between theory and practice in actual process of marriage and family therapy. There are two crucial parts of competence for the family therapist. The first involves recognizing the limits of one's expertise and experience. As therapists we are in the role of the expert. Our expertise is essential if we are to help our clients. Yet it is easy to move beyond the limits of our expertise and not even be aware of it. Marriage and family therapists are responsible for recognizing and being aware of the limits of their expertise. The second crucial aspect of competence involves a responsibility to continually expand our knowledge and skills. Our discipline is continually expanding and we have a responsibility to be engaged in a continual growth process. We should not overlook the fact that our clients have a great deal to teach us. The virtue of competence relates to trust. Our clients will not be able to trust us unless we practice our profession in a competent and respectful way.

The next virtue is diligence. The clinician is responsible for pursuing work with clients, to the best of his or her ability. In Aristotelian terms, the clinician aims at excellence (areté—virtue). Practicing diligence involves setting limits on the number of clients seen and the number of hours worked. Our responsibility is to set for ourselves appropriate boundaries. An essential aspect of diligence is the ability to discipline oneself. Self-discipline comes from within rather than being imposed from outside by one's professional organization. Indeed, our profession requires a commitment to rigorous academic and clinical training. This training requires self-discipline and the ability to delay gratification. Many of the issues that come to our ethics committees involve, at least in part, a lack of self-control and self-discipline. A marriage and family therapist is diligent in his or her work and this involves a high degree of self-discipline.

The fourth virtue is loyalty. The therapist is loyal to his or her clients. The therapist keeps the client's best interests as a primary consideration in the practice of family therapy. In private practice loyalty issues are for the most part simple because there are only two parties to the therapeutic contract. Yet many family therapists work for agencies and in that sense are also employers. In these more complicated contexts, issues around "split loyalties" can occur. Codes of ethics cannot give us a preset formula on how to resolve situations in which we find ourselves pulled in different directions by conflicting loyalties. Often, "split loyalty" issues arise from dual relationships. One argument against dual relationships is that it can give rise to situations in which the clinician is caught in conflicting loyalties.

The fifth virtue that Bayles describes is the virtue of discretion. Discretion is a broader concept than confidentiality because it includes material that is not confidential. The underlying value is privacy which involves control of information about oneself that others have. Discretion involves judgment as to what to discuss and what not to discuss. Discretion also can involve an element of timing. Since discretion involves discernment and judgment, it cannot be defined and specified in advance. Discretion is part of respecting clients and the boundaries of a professional relationship.

The five virtues just described were formulated by Michael Bayles in the broader context of his examination of professional life in general. Our examination has focused on how these virtues are essential to the work of the marriage and family therapist. Yet we are left with a question: "Are there other virtues that apply specifically to the practice of family therapy?"

There are three additional virtues that are important for family therapists. The first virtue, collegiality, while not unique to family therapy, is crucial to our work. MacIntyre has compellingly argued that professionals are a part of a community of practice. Even if a therapist works in a private practice, he or she is still part of a discipline whose knowledge and skills were not developed in isolation. Family therapists have a responsibility to work with other therapists and other professionals for the well-being of clients. Our community of practice relates to other health-related communities of practice. We have a responsibility to collaborate with other professionals and to do so in a collegial manner.

Another virtue for family therapists is sensitivity. Our work as therapists involves people. As therapists we need to be sensitive to the feelings, relationships, and self-esteem of our clients and colleagues. Sensitivity is one of the ingredients of a trustful relationship.

A final virtue for the marriage and family therapist is curiosity. The nature of our work involves knowledge and expertise, but our knowledge becomes stale and eventually dead if it is not accompanied by a curiosity about our own lives as well as those of our clients. We help clients get unstuck; we are in the business of evoking "possibilities." Our own imaginations are an important part of what we do as therapists. Curiosity involves an ongoing desire to learn. In this sense the virtue of curiosity overlaps the virtue of competence. Both curiosity and competence are ongoing processes rather than fixed states. Curiosity and imagination lead therapists to discover new insights and skills in working with couples and families.

In effect all eight of these virtues go to make up a good and healthy therapeutic relationship; one that involves personal integrity and respect for clients from the therapist's perspective and one that is competent, caring, and trustworthy from the client's point of view. These eight virtues that we have identified and explored make up the hierarchy of values for the profession of marriage and family therapy. Every profession serves an overriding norm (law serves justice, teaching serves knowledge, medicine serves health) and marriage and family therapy serves the norms of wholeness and healthy relationships.

The practice of marriage and family therapy resides within the tension between individual well-being and healthy relationships. Viewed from the individual perspective, we work with individuals and their emotional, social, and moral well-being. This well-being cannot exist in isolation because our individual well-being is inextricably interwoven into our significant relationships. The moral issue, from the individualistic perspective, is the issue of integrity, i.e., of moral wholeness. As therapists we seek a type of integrity that includes both masculine and feminine dimensions of integrity. John Beebe, in his book *Integrity in Depth*, explores a vision of integrity that transcends the stereotypes of gender roles with which we have been raised.[5] Carl Jung provides the best theoretical basis from which to do this work with his concepts of animus (the underdeveloped male side of the female) and the anima (the underdeveloped feminine side of the male). Jung theorizes that in midlife the developmental task is for the woman to develop her masculine aspect while the man develops his feminine aspects. As therapists we need a vision of integrity—moral wholeness which honors sexual differences and transcends the stereotypes of restrictive gender roles which inhibit individual as well as relational growth and development.

From the relational side the norm of wholeness takes on the form of healthy relationships. The British psychoanalyst Winnicott thought of therapy as the receptive holding of a client and the client's issues. Barbara Sullivan has described this attitude as "psychotherapy grounded in the feminine principle."[6] John Beebe

---

[5]Beebe, John. "Integrity and Gender." In *Integrity in Depth*, ed. John Beebe. College Station TX: Texas A&M University Press, 1992, 70–98.

[6]Sullivan, Barbara. *Psychotherapy Grounded in Feminine Principle*. Wilmmette IL: Chiron, 1989.

maintains that a feminine notion of constancy plays a crucial role in the development of the self and in the process of therapy.[7] As therapists we work in a relational medium that until recently had been reserved for women. The basis for constancy in a relationship is a sense of mutual trust. As Sissela Bok pointed out earlier, whatever we experience as valuable occurs in an atmosphere of trust. Healthy relationships are based upon constancy and trust. Family therapists operate on the interrelated norms of wholeness and healthy relationships.

Now that I have clearly defined virtue for the marriage and family therapist, it is important to address an old yet still critical question: "Can virtue be taught?"

CAN VIRTUE BE TAUGHT?

My examination of virtue leads us back to the central issue of the last chapter, the issue of moral development. In the *Republic,* Socrates examines the issue of the virtue of justice and raises the question: "Can this virtue as well as the other virtues be taught?" Plato's conclusions, that he attributes to Socrates, are less important than the legacy of the method of Socratic questioning and of the rational search for the moral dimension within the context of the good life.

Reflecting on virtues takes us back from behaviors to an examination of our attitudes and motives. With this shift in mind, Iris Murdock describes three obstacles to moral living.[8] The first is our preoccupation with our "selves" and our

---

[7]Austin, Jane. *Persuasion*. New York: Bantam, 1984, 207–210.

[8]Murdock, Iris. "On God and Good." In *Revisions: Changing Perspectives in Moral Philosophy*, ed. Stanley Hauerwas and Alasdair MacIntyre. South Bend: University of Notre Dame Press, 1983, 72.

projects. We have a persistent inability to step outside our own egos and to see what else is going on in the world. The second obstacle is the inability to recognize and focus on the moral dimension. This is both an awareness of the moral dimension—an issue of moral diagnosis, i.e., recognizing a moral issue—as well as a lack of moral knowledge. Human moral beliefs are often found to be sadly lacking when closely examined. Murdock thinks that our final obstacle is a lack of attention to the "good." We need clear visions of what constitutes the "good" and what makes up healthy relationships. Without a positive moral vision we can easily get caught up in and remain within the psychological realm. The task of the family therapist involves a commitment to a continuing process of moral self-understanding (while avoiding excessive scrupulosity) which involves an examination of one's motives as well as a study of the virtues of the moral life and an awareness of the human egocentric predicament. The answer to the question, "Can virtue be taught?" is that virtue can be taught only if the other person wants to learn. Mary Waithe and David Ozar, in *The Ethics of Teaching Ethics*, describe the case of a physician who both sexually molested and defrauded patients.[9] The physician was required to take a course in professional ethics. Waithe and Ozar point out that intellectual mastery of ethical theory and the virtuous practice of medicine, while related, are still quite different. In this case it could be unethical to teach ethics because it may contribute to the illusion that the physician is a responsible professional, when, as a matter of fact, he has no intention of acquiring an attitude of respect for his patients and behaving in respectful ways.

---

[9]Waithe, Mary and David Ozar. "The Ethics of Teaching Ethics." *Hastings Center Report*, 1990, 17–21.

In our quest for virtue we need to be careful that we are not overcome by our concern for the good. As Carl Jung pointed out by means of his concept of the "shadow," we all have a side of ourselves which is selfish, mean, cruel, vengeful, and arrogant—the irrational side of our emotional lives. Recognition and acceptance of this aspect of our personalities is in itself a moral problem. John Beebe points out that, "The acceptance by the self of its own failures to achieve its ideals is the only way that it can earn the empathy required for a human attitude toward the shadow."[10]

While virtue can't be taught, then, in the strict sense of "teaching," relevant ethical theory, a knowledge of the virtues required for the practice of family therapy, and a discussion of the motives and dilemmas involved in practicing marriage and family therapy, can be parts of a context in which experiential leaning about ethics and the development of character can take place. The isomorphism is apparent at this point—we can't force our clients to grow, but we can act as catalysts in the process. As therapists we have the responsibility to act as catalysts in the moral development of couples and families with whom we work, as well as with ourselves and our colleagues. What we are pursuing was clearly pointed out by Aristotle:

> Every art and every inquiry and similarly every action and pursuit is thought to aim at some good; and for this reason the good has rightly been declared to be that at which all things aim (Book I, Section I0)....Therefore, if this is true in every case, the virtue of man also will be the state of character which

---

[10]Beebe, John. "Integrity and Gender." In *Integrity in Depth*, ed. John Beebe. College Station TX: Texas A&M University Press, 1992, 65.

makes a man good and which makes him do his work well (Book II, Section 6).[11]

Much of Western ethics is based upon a rational approach to ethics, which was first articulated by Aristotle. Many moral philosophers have differed from Aristotle in terms of content, yet, nonetheless, have worked on a reason-based approach to ethics. Aristotle, too, had his shadow side. He divided human beings into two classes: Greeks and Barbarians. Reason-based approaches to ethics culminate in Kant, who wrote, "Nor could one give poorer counsel to morality than to attempt to derive it from examples....".[12]

Aristotle, however, advises that if one would know the good and wish to become good, he or she should watch what a good person does. Max Scheler, the German phenomenologist, and Henri Bergson, the French philosopher, both give primary importance to moral experience and to moral models. For Plato, Socrates is the moral paradigm. Philosophers, as well as religious communities, have their saints who are exemplars of the good life lived with moral excellence. Thus, a physician wishing to practice morally should not get his or her theories from moral philosophers but rather from a virtuous physician who serves as a model. This leads us back to Robert Coles and his insight that families develop character which is in part based upon children imitating the moral models that they observe.

Case
All of our previous cases have involved a variety of *moral dilemmas*. An example of a *moral model* is appropriate at this point. In the fall of 1989 the author heard Augustus Napier speak at the annual meeting of the American

---

[11]Aristotle. "Nichomachean Ethics." In *The Oxford Translation of Aristotle*, ed. W. D. Ross. Oxford: Oxford University Press, 1925.

[12]Kant, Immanuel. "The Groundwork of the Metaphysics of Morality." In *Morality and the Good Life*, ed. Robert Solomon. New York: McGraw-Hill, 1984, 261.

Association of Marriage and Family Therapists. Napier addressed the issue of marriage in our society through the lens of his own experience and marriage. Napier had mastered the theory of marital therapy and had acquired considerable skill at the practice of marital therapy over almost two decades of practice. Napier believed that he and his wife had a good marriage. Then one day he asked her—only to receive a shocking answer— that she felt much more negative about their marriage. This question opened up new and difficult ground for them as a couple. Napier began the process of coming to terms with his own shadow while at the same time they came to grips with the shadow side of their marriage. Napier's willingness to be this vulnerable in front of four thousand of his colleagues was both remarkable as well as inspirational. Napier provides us with a model of a clinician who struggles to learn and grow with his clients and at the same time engage in his own growth within his marriage, and most importantly, to allow growth in one area to penetrate the other. Napier has reflected on his experience in his book, *The Fragile Bond: In Search of An Equal, Intimate, and Enduring Marriage.*[13]

VIRTUES AND THE MORAL COMMUNITY

The virtues we have examined, and the models we have suggested, exist, as Aristotle pointed out, within communities. It is important to examine virtue within the communal and cultural contexts in which they are practiced.

Philip Reiff, in *The Triumph of the Therapeutic*, analyzes psychotherapy as a cultural phenomenon.[14] From a sociological perspective Reiff distinguishes between commitment and analytic therapies. Commitment therapies are authoritarian in nature in that they require belief in their theory and approach. Primal therapy in the 1970s, neurolinguistic programming in the 1980s, and now multiple personality disorder theory, each claim to achieve central insight into human beings and how they can be healed. These are but three examples of many such approaches. Each

---

[13]Napier, Augustus Y. *The Fragile Bond: In Search of an Equal, Intimate and Enduring Marriage.* New York: Harper & Row, 1988.

[14]Reiff, Philip. *The Triumph of the Therapeutic.* New York: Harper & Row, 1966.

new approach tends to gather adherents who maintain that we now have the key needed to do therapeutic work. Commitment therapies require belief in the theory and generate disciples. In contrast, analytic therapies take an anti-authoritarian stance. By paying the fee the client discharges his or her debt of gratitude to the therapist. The disciple, in contrast, always remains in debt to his or her mentor. Reiff credits Freud with moving therapy from a religious base which seeks a cure to the analytic model which has for its goal the expansion of the client's freedom. In the psychoanalytic view the price of civilization is the development of neurosis in the individual. The psychoanalytic model sees the individual as emotionally buried alive in a crippled way in the culture.

Psychoanalysis seeks the liberation of the client. The missing dimension of this model is that there is no healthy community to which the individual can return and participate in healthy relationships. An exception to this is the Jungian approach to psychoanalysis which clearly requires a community of believers in Jungian theory. This approach, while describing itself as "analytic," is in Reiff's terms actually a commitment type of therapy. The analytic approach nonetheless exists at the end of a long line of paradigms that have an individualistic framework. In "Socrates and Psychotherapy" I have traced the evolution of this paradigm from Socrates to Freud.[15]

I maintain that these paradigms, while important to the development of therapy, are inadequate for marriage and family therapists because of their individualistic frameworks. Reiff's contribution is his attempt to understand therapy

---

[15]Lageman, August. "Socrates and Psychotherapy." *Journal of Religion and Health* 28 (3) (Fall 1989): 219–223.

within a theory of culture. Reiff maintains that therapy cannot be understood as an isolated phenomenon, but that therapeutic theories and systems are a cultural phenomenon.

Another sociologist, Erving Goffman, analyzes therapeutic interactions in terms of the roles that the self plays.[16] For Goffman the unit of analysis is the individual role-player striving to effect his or her will within a role-structured situation. For Goffman the new role on the twentieth century stage is the role of the therapist.

Alasdair MacIntyre combines a sociological/cultural analysis with an historical perspective in his chapter "Why the Enlightenment Project of Justifying Morality Had to Fail." MacIntyre traces the Enlightenment's attempt to ground morality on a national basis.[17] Prior to the Enlightenment, morality had often been grounded in religious faith, but reason destroyed that basis. During the time of the Enlightenment, David Hume attempted to ground morality in our emotions. For Hume, and later for Henry Sidwick and Adam Smith, morality was a matter of having moral sentiments from which moral behavior arose. Grounding morality in emotions failed because it left us with a subjective foundation for ethics. Kant's grand attempt to ground morality in reason and in universal principles also failed because his ethical system, while coherent and forceful, failed to achieve universal acceptance and has its own problems (as we have seen, with ethical issues involving attachment issues where impartiality does not apply).

---

[16]Goffman, Erving. *The Presentation of Self in Everyday Life.* Garden City: Doubleday, 1959.

[17]MacIntyre, Alasdair. *After Virtue.* South Bend: Notre Dame University Press, 1981, 55–61.

MacIntyre points out "...the individual moral agent, freed from hierarchy and teleology, conceives of himself and is conceived of by moral philosophers as *sovereign* in his moral authority."[18] MacIntyre describes how this sovereignty has left us with a paradox:

> Contemporary moral experience as a consequence has a paradoxical character. For each of us is taught to see himself or herself as an autonomous moral agent; but each of us also becomes engaged by modes of practice, aesthetic or bureaucratic, which involve us in manipulative relationships with others. Seeking to protect the autonomy that we have learned to prize, we aspire ourselves *not* to be manipulated by others; seeking to incarnate our own principles and standpoint in the world of practice, we find no way open to us to do so except by directing towards others those very manipulative modes of relationship which each of us aspires to resist in our own case. The incoherence of our attitudes and our experience arises from the incoherent conceptual scheme which we have inherited.[19]

Thus we are left with the legacy of the Enlightenment as ourselves as morally sovereign and autonomous individuals, but without a secure moral grounding for our moral beliefs, theories, and practices. In practical times we are left with the ethical relativism that we see in our clients and students. The prevailing view is that one ethical belief is as good as another.

Thus, we end up with either ethical relativism or believing that our own ethical beliefs and theories are the sole possessors of the truth. We then spend time defending our moral and therapeutic ideologies, and critical analysis and synthesis are not possible. There is a parallel process between the truth claims of each of the major approaches to moral philosophy and the truth claims of each of the major therapeutic schools. In moral philosophy the deontologists attack the utilitarians and

---

[18]*ibid.*, 62.

[19]*ibid.*, 68.

so on, while in family systems approaches the strategic therapists and the structural

therapists attack one another. MacIntyre describes the paralyzing effect of this

process of attack and counterattack:

> The therapist by contrast is not only the most liable of the three typical
> characters of modernity to be deceived [the aesthete, the manager, and the
> therapist], but is also the most liable to be seen to be deceived, and not only
> by moral fictions. Devastating hostile critiques of the standard therapeutic
> theories of our culture are easily available; indeed each school of therapists
> is all too anxious to make clear the theoretical defects of each rival school.
> Thus the problem is not why the claims of psychoanalytic or behavior
> therapies are not exposed as ill founded; it is rather, why, since they have
> been so adequately undermined, the practices of therapy continue for the
> most part as though nothing had happened.[20]

With these ideological wars raging, both in moral philosophy and the

therapeutic professions, we are left with little time and energy to construct moral

and therapeutic visions of human wholeness.

From the analysis in this chapter, family therapists are left with a fourfold task

as we integrate moral dimension with marriage and family therapy. The first issue

that arises from within "systematic" approaches is to successfully overcome the

individualism inherent in most of our moral theories and beliefs. The second area of

responsibility is to continue to promote ideals for our profession while recognizing

that there is a "shadow" side to our idealism. The third aspect of our responsibility

is the ongoing issue of the grounding of our moral theories and beliefs. The final

aspect of our fourfold task is to do a critical analysis of our own profession from

historical, cultural, and sociological perspectives. This analysis was begun in the

first chapter of this book.

---

[20]*ibid.*, 72–73.

In this chapter I have identified and described eight virtues for the marriage and family therapist. These virtues are, in effect, a hierarchy of values for our profession. They make up the "internal goods" of our moral lives. I have argued that the moral life is better cultivated internally by a virtue-based approach than by concentrating on externally required behaviors. The virtues that I have described are the internal moral goods that we need to relate to our clients in trustful and therapeutic ways. I have argued, on an Aristotelian basis, that virtues can only be made sense of, as well as practiced, in relationships and communities. The Greeks recognized that there is an inseparable relationship between being a good person and being a good citizen.

The goal of marriage and family therapy is healthy relationships. Healthy relationships are "whole" emotionally, relationally, and morally. Ethically speaking, our goal is respect for persons. Ethically and therapeutically, our goals converge. This goal can only be attained in communities which recognize and respect the moral dimensions of human relationships.

Chapter 7
Conclusion

In the previous chapter I have examined the virtues that the family therapist practices in working with clients. Viewed therapeutically this involves examining the "person" or "character" of the therapist. Work is going on within marriage and family therapy to understand the different "postures" that therapists adopt in their work with couples and families.

KARL TOMM'S APPROACH

Karl Tomm is working on identifying and clarifying the various postures that therapists adopt in their work with couples and families.[1] Tomm begins with the possibility of opening space with people (defined as loving people) or closing space for people (described as imposing one's will on another—violence). The second aspect of Tomm's approach revolves around whether or not the therapist's interventions are conscious or not. With both of these aspects four possibilities emerge.

---

[1]Tomm, Karl. "Ethical Postures That Orient One's Decision Making." AFTA Meeting, 1990. Audio tape.

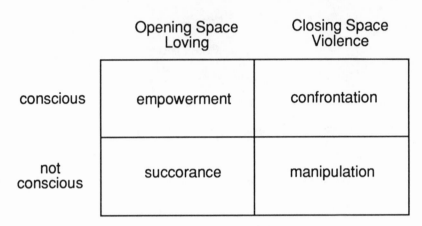

FIGURE 2: KARL TOMM'S "SPACES"

In the manipulative quadrant the therapist deceives the client in ways the client is not aware of, thereby closing space for the client. The therapist is acting to reduce options. This may be necessary in certain situations, for example, in hospitalizing a suicidal client. The strategic approach of Jay Haley tends to operate from this quadrant.[2] Working from a manipulative posture produces the effects of deference and even subservience in clients.

In the confrontational quadrant the therapist intervenes on a conscious level to reduce the options of clients and pushes them to a desired outcome. The structural approach of Salvador Minuchin operates from this quadrant.[3] Confrontational approaches tend to produce concessions with compliance.

---

[2]Haley, Jay. *Strategies of Psychotherapy*. New York: Grune and Stratton, 1963.

[3]Minuchin, Salvador. *Families and Family Therapy*. Cambridge: Harvard University Press, 1974.

In the empowering approach the therapist operates at a conscious level to open space for clients. The therapist is actively encouraging and is working to evoke new options and possibilities for clients. The work of David Epstom and Michael White fall into this quadrant.[4] Working from an empowering posture with clients tends to produce liberation and autonomy.

The final approach is the succorant posture. In this approach the client receives but is not aware of the therapist's emotional messages. A non-therapeutic example of this is children being nurtured without being aware of what is going on. This approach nourishes clients. The Milan approach works primarily from this quadrant.[5] Operating from this posture produces both growth for the client and dependence on the therapist.

Tomm stresses that the effects of the therapist's interventions are not determined by the intentions of the therapist, but on the client's experience of the intervention. Tomm stresses the values of not knowing, of curiosity, and of changing one's mind for the therapist. He maintains that we should give priority to experience over explanations and not assume that the therapist's truth is better than the client's truth.

Tomm opens up an additional axis involving whether the therapist operates as an expert with the aura of professional and personal secrecy (the analytic incognito) or is open about himself or herself. Here there are four ways in which to view clients. If we describe clients as resistant we will tend to take stances that

---

[4]Epstom, David and Michael White. *Narrative Means to Therapeutic Ends*. New York: Norton Press, 1990.

[5]Boscolo, Luigi, Grantanco Cecchin, Lynn Hoffman, and Peggy Penn. *Milan Systemic Family Therapy*. New York: Basic Books, 1987.

necessitate manipulative interventions. Our temptation at this point is to "blame" the client. On the other hand, if we believe clients to be mistaken, deviant, wrong, and abnormal, we may easily adopt a stance that uses confrontational responses. If we view clients as oppressed by their problems, we will tend to operate in empowering ways to open space for them. If we believe clients to be stuck and naive we tend to operate in succorant ways.

Tomm's therapeutic postures are moral stances from which we interact with our clients. Each posture involves an attitude toward clients. Manipulative and confrontational stances are paternalistic and there are times when we should act from these stances. I maintain, however, that these times are the exceptions and that our usual postures should be empowering and nurturing—in effect loving our clients. The atmosphere in the therapy room is critical. Furthermore, I maintain that family therapists should be conscious of their postures and attitudes toward clients. This relates to the virtues that I have identified in the previous chapters.

Family therapists should, for example, practice virtues such as curiosity and sensitivity. Clearly, such virtues need to be conscious in the mind of the therapist. We must be aware of and know our own postures and beliefs that we have about our work and our clients.

CONCLUSION

I began this book with the recognition that marriage and family therapy is a value-laden activity which focuses on relationships and patterns of interaction, and is, therefore, involved in moral issues. This book has examined marriage and family through a variety of moral paradigms.

The first case raised the issue, "What right do therapists have to attempt to change clients' value systems?" I maintain that while we need to be clear about our own values as well as speaking out against values that dehumanize others, it is crucial for our work as therapists that we help our clients see their moral dilemmas in the context of their own value systems.

I then moved on to consider the wider social, political, and ideological contexts in which we practice family therapy. Family therapists have a responsibility to work to overcome the bifurcation of life into private and public realms. We need to work against the social and political structures which foster prejudice and violence. Marriage and family therapists have a responsibility to work for a balance of power in human affairs that is best described as justice. I have argued for a broad context in which to consider our work. The stakeholders (interested and affected parties) are our clients, our profession, and the world community.

Three broader areas of moral requirements for marriage and family therapists have emerged from an examination of the AAMFT Code of Ethics, its limitations, and from dilemmas clinicians are currently facing. The first is our responsibility to deal with the dilemmas that arise from gender, ethnic, cultural, and religious differences. A fundamental dilemma occurs in the conflict between individual and family perspectives. Our second responsibility is to be aware of the relativity of our belief systems as well as the limits of our own knowledge. Finally, it is of critical importance to recognize and work with the ethical dimensions of the therapeutic contract.

I have examined the issues generated from the practice of marriage and family therapy from four different approaches to moral philosophy: from the point of view of the therapists' duties; an examination of family therapy from the client's vantage point—client rights; then a correlation of client rights with therapist duties; an application of developmental moral theory; and, finally, I considered a virtue-based approach to marriage and family therapy. I conducted this fourfold application of moral philosophy to marriage and family therapy for two reasons. The first was to integrate both disciplines and the second reason was to shed light on the moral conflicts and dilemmas that we face as marriage and family therapists.

In chapter six I examined the virtue-based approach to ethics, identifying eight virtues for the marriage and family therapist. These virtues are the "internal goods" of our profession and are needed to practice and work with our clients in trustful and respectful ways. The virtue-based approach brought us the "person" of the therapy. With the help of Karl Tomm I analyzed the different postures or stances that family therapists take with their clients. I maintain that these postures have a moral dimension to them. Indeed, everything we do as marriage and family therapists has a moral dimension to it.

Education is the activation of one's moral imagination. Hopefully, the interaction of moral theory with clinical practice has done this for the reader. At the same time, I recognize that theory, no matter how good it is, is irrelevant unless there is an awareness of and sensitivity to the moral dimensions of our lives and work. I hope this book has helped to foster the recognition and diagnosis of moral issues in marriage and family therapy.

Bibliography

Abate, Luciano L. and Gerald R. Weeks. *Paradoxical Psychotherapy*. New York: Brunner Mazel, 1982.
_____."Professional and Ethical Issues." In *Paradoxical Psychotherapy*. New York: Brunno Mazel, 1982.

Anderson, Carol. *The Therapeutic Contract*. Family Therapy Network Symposium, Washington, D.C., 1987. Audio tape.

Aristotle. *The Nichomachean Ethics*. Book V, Chapter III. Translated by J. A. K. Thompson. London: Penguin Books, 1976.

Aronfreed, Justin. *Conduct and Conscience*. New York: Academic Press, 1968.

Austin, Jane. *Persuasion*. New York: Bantam, 1984.

Bader, Ellyn and Peter Pearson. *In Quest of the Mythical Mate: A Developmental Approach to Diagnosis and Treatment in Couples Therapy*. New York: Brunner Mazel, 1988.

Barry, Vincent. *Applying Ethics: A Text With Readings*. 2d ed. Belmont: Wadsworth Publishing Co., 1985.

Bayles, Michael D. "Ethics of Limited Knowledge in the Healing Professions." In *Professional Ethics in Health Care Services*, ed. Eugene Kelly. New York: University Press of America, 1988.
_____. *Professional Ethics*. 2d ed. Belmont CA: Wadsworth Publishing Co., 1989.
_____. "Trust and the Professional-Client Relationship." In *Professional Ideals*, ed. Albert Flores. Belmont CA: Wadsworth Publishing Co., 1988, 66–79.

Beebe, John. "Integrity and Gender." In *Integrity in Depth*, ed. John Beebe. College Station TX: Texas A&M University Press, 1992.

Bledstein, Burton. *The Culture of Professionalism*. New York: Norton, 1976.

Bledstein, Burton. *Models for Ethical Medicine in A Revolutionary Age*. Briarcliff Manor NY: Hastings Center, 1976.

Bly, Robert. *Men and the Wound—The Naive Male*. St. Paul: Ally Press, 1988.

Bok, Sissela. *Lying: Moral Choice in Public and Private Life*. New York: Random House, 1978.
_____. *Secrets: On the Ethics of Concealment and Revelation*. New York: Random House, 1983.

Boscolo, Luigi, Grantanco Cecchin, Lynn Hoffman, and Peggy Penn. *Milan Systemic Family Therapy*. New York: Basic Books, 1987.

Code of Ethical Principles for Marriage and Family Therapists. The American Association of Marriage and Family Therapists. Washington, D.C., 1991.

Collins, Randall. *The Credentialed Society*. New York: Academic Press, 1979.

Counseling Services: Consumer Rights and Responsibilities. The National Board of Certified Counselors, Alexandria VA.

Cusa, A. S. *Dimensions of Moral Creativity*. University Park: The Pennsylvania State University Press, 1978.

Darwall, Stephen. "Two Kinds of Respect." *Ethics* 88 (1977).

Dyer, Allen. *Ethics in Psychiatry: Toward Professional Definition*. Washington D.C.: American Psychiatric Press, 1988.

Edwards, C. P. "Cross-Cultural Research on Kohlberg's Stages: The Basis for Consensus." In *Lawrence Kohlberg, Consensus and Controversy*, ed. S. Modgil and C. Modgil. Lewes, U. K.: Falmer Press, 1985, 419–430.

Epstom, David and Michael White. *Narrative Means to Therapeutic Ends*. New York: Norton Press, 1990.

Eysenck, H. J. *Fact and Fiction in Psychology*. Harmondsworth: Penguin Books, 1965.

Feinberg, Joel. "The Nature and Value of Rights." In *The Philosophy of Human Rights*, ed. Morton Winston. Belmont CA: Wadsworth Publishing Co., 1989, 61–74.

Flores, Albert. *Professional Ideals*. Belmont CA: Wadsworth Publishing Co., 1988.

Gilligan, Carol. *In A Different Voice*. Cambridge MA: Harvard University Press, 1982.

Goffman, Erving. *The Presentation of Self in Everyday Life*. Garden City: Doubleday, 1959.

Goldman, Alan H. *The Moral Foundations of Professional Ethics*. Totowa NJ: Roman and Littlefield, 1980.

Goode, William. "Community Within a Community." *American Sociological Review* XXII (1957): 194.

Green, Susan and James Hansen. "Ethical Dilemmas Faced by Family Therapists." *Journal of Marriage and Family Therapy* 2 (1989): 149–158.

Griffin, Susan. "A Chorus of Stones: The Private Life of War." Book yet to be published.

Guggenbuhl-Craig, Adolf. *Power in the Helping Professions*. Irving TX: Spring Publications, 1979.

Haas, Peter J. *Morality After Auschwitz: The Radical Challenge of the Nazi Ethic*. Philadelphia: Fortress Press, 1988.

Haley, Jay. *Problem-Solving Therapy*. 2d ed. San Francisco: Jossey-Bass, 1987.
_____. *Strategies of Psychotherapy*. New York: Grune and Stratton, 1963.

Hauerwas, Stanley. *Vision and Virtue*. Notre Dame IN: Fides Publishers, 1974.

Henderson, Michael C. "Paradoxical Process and Ethical Consciousness." *Family Therapy* 3 (1987): 191.

The Moral Dimensions of Marriage and Family Therapy

Herman, Barbara. "Agency, Attachment, and Difference." *Ethics* 101 (1991).

Kanigel, Robert. "The Endangered Professional." *Johns Hopkins Magazine*, 1988, 1.

Kant, Immanuel. *Groundwork of the Metaphysic of Morals.* Translated by H. J. Paton. New York: Harper & Row, 1964.

Keith-Spregel, Patricia and Gerald P. Koocher. *Ethics in Psychology: Professional Standards and Cases.* New York: Random House, 1985.

Kiefer, Christie W. *The Mantle of Maturity: A History of Ideas About Character Development.* Albany: State University of New York Press, 1988.

Kohlberg, Lawrence. *Essays on Moral Development.* Vol. I. San Francisco: Harper and Row, 1984.

Kuhn, Thomas S. *The Structure of Scientific Revolutions.* 2d ed. Chicago: University of Chicago Press, 1970.

Kultgen, John. *Ethics and Professionalism.* Philadelphia: University of Pennsylvania Press, 1988.
_____. "The Ideological Use of Professional Codes." *Business and Professional Ethics Journal* 1 (Spring 1982): 53–69.

Lageman, August. "Encounter With Death: The Thought of Robert Jay Lifton." *Journal of Religion and Health* Winter 26 (1987): 300–308.
_____. "Socrates and Psychotherapy." *Journal of Religion and Health* 28 (Fall 1989): 219–223.
_____. "The Moral Lives of Children: The Thought of Robert Coles." *Journal of Religion and Health* 29 (1990): 303–307.

Larson, Magali Sarfatti. *The Rise of Professionalism.* Berkeley: University of California Press, 1977.

Lebacqz, Karen. *Professional Ethics: Power and Paradox.* Nashville: Abingdon Press, 1985.

Lifton, Robert Jay. *The Nazi Doctors: Medical Killing and the Psychology of Genocide.* New York: Basic Books, 1986.

London, Perry. *The Modes and Morals of Psychotherapy.* 2d ed. New York: McGraw-Hill, 1986.

Lyons, Nona P. "Two Perspectives: One Self, Relationships, and Morality." *Harvard Educational Review* 53 (1983): 124–125.

MacIntyre, Alasdair. *After Virtue.* South Bend: Notre Dame University Press, 1981.

Magoli, Larson. *The Rise of Professionalism.* Berkeley CA: University of California Press, 1977.

May, William. "The Beleaguered Rulers: The Public Obligations of the Professionals." *Kennedy Institute of Ethics Journal* 2 (1992): 25–41.

Miller, Alice. *For Your Own Good: Hidden Cruelty in Child Rearing and the Roots of Violence.* Translated by Hannum, Hildegaard and Hunter. New York: Farrar, Straus, and Geroux, 1983.

Minuchin, Salvador. *Families and Family Therapy.* Cambridge: Harvard University Press, 1974.

Mount, Eric. *Professional Ethics in Context.* Louisville: Westminster/John Knox Press, 1990.

Murdock, Iris. "On God and Good." In *Revisions: Changing Perspectives in Moral Philosophy,* ed. Stanley Hauerwas and Alasdair MacIntyre. South Bend: University of Notre Dame Press, 1983, 72.

Napier, Augustus Y. *The Fragile Bond: In Search of an Equal, Intimate and Enduring Marriage.* New York: Harper & Row, 1988.

Neill, John R. *From Psyche to System: The Evolving Therapy of Carl Whitaker.* ed. David Kniskein. New York: Guilford Press, 1982.

Nichols, Michael. *The Self in the System: Expanding the Limits of Family Therapy*. New York: Brunner Mazel, 1987.

Ogletree, Thomas W. *Hospitality to the Stranger: Dimensions of Moral Understanding*. Philadelphia: Fortress Press, 1985.

Perry, William. *Forms of Intellectual and Ethical Development in the College Years*. New York: Holt, Rinehart, and Winston, 1970.

Pope, Kenneth and Melba Vasquez. *Ethics in Counseling and Psychotherapy*. San Francisco: Jossey-Bass Publishers, 1991.

"Public Duties of the Professions." Briarcliff Manor NY: *Hastings Center Report*, 1987.

Ratliff, Nancy. *A Workbook for Ethical Decision Making*. El Paso: Montgomery Methods, 1988.

Rawls, John. *A Theory of Justice*. London: Oxford University Press, 1972.

Reiff, Philip. *The Triumph of the Therapeutic*. New York: Harper & Row, 1966.

Riceour, Paul. *Freud and Philosophy*. New Haven: Yale University Press, 1970.

Rorty, Richard. *Contingency, Irony, and Solidarity*. New York: Cambridge University, 1989.

Ross, William D. *The Right and The Good*. Oxford: Clarendon Press, 1930.

Ryder, Robert and Jeri Hepworth. "AAMFT Ethical Code: 'Dual Relationships'." *Journal of Marital and Family Therapy* 16 (April 1990): 127–132.

Shue, Henry. "Security and Subsistence." In *The Philosophy of Human Rights*, ed. Morton Winston. Belmont CA: Wadsworth Publishing Co., 1989, 152–171.

Solomon, Robert. *A Passion for Justice: Emotions and the Origins of the Social Contract*. New York: Addison Wesley, 1990.

Sommers, Christina. "Teaching the Virtues." *American Philosophical Newsletter*, 1991, 42.

Sullivan, Barbara. *Psychotherapy Grounded in Feminine Principle.* Wilmmette IL: Chiron, 1989.

The Teaching of Ethics in Higher Education. The Hastings Center, 255 Elm Road, Briarcliff Manyor, N.Y., 1980.

Tomm, Karl. "Ethical Postures That Orient One's Decision Making." AFTA Meeting, 1990.

Veatch, Robert. *A Theory of Medical Ethics.* New York: Basic Books, 1981.
_____. *Models for Ethical Medicine in A Revolutionary Age.* Briarcliff Manor NY: Hastings Center, 1972.

Vine, Ian. "Moral Maturity in Socio-Cultural Perspective: Are Kohlberg's Stages Universal?" In *Lawrence Kohlberg, Consensus and Controversy*, ed. S. Modgil and C. Modgil. Lewes U.K.: Falmer Press, 1985, 431–450.

Waithe, Mary and David Ozar. "The Ethics of Teaching Ethics." *Hastings Center Report*, 1990.

Werhane, Patricia. "Individual Rights in Business." In *Just Business*, ed. Tom Regan. New York: Random House, 1984, 120.

Winston, Morton. *The Philosophy of Human Rights.* Belmont CA: Wadsworth Publishing Co., 1989.

Zygmond, Mary Jo and Harriet Boorhem. "Ethical Decision Making in Family Therapy." *Family Process* 28 (Sept 1989).

Minuchin, Salvador, 106

Mount, Eric, 8, 9, 15

Murdock, Iris, 95, 96

Napier, Augustus, 98

Nichols, Michael, 29

Nietzsche, Friedrich, v

Ogletree, Thomas, 2

Ozar, David, 96

Pearson, Peter, 35

Perry, William, 39

Piaget, Jean, 70

Plato, 16, 53, 95, 98

Price, David, 9

Pulliom, Martha, 15

Quayle, Dan, 15

Ratliff, Nancy, 20, 27

Rawls, John, 75

Reiff, Philip, 99, 100, 101

Ross, W. D., 45, 46, 60, 61, 62

Rousseau, Jean Jacques, 53

Ryder, Robert, 21, 26

Scheler, Max, 98

Shue, Henry, 58

Sidwick, Henry, 101

Skinner, B. F., 69

Smith, Adam, 101

Socrates, 32, 95, 98, 100

Sommers, Christina, 39

Sullivan, Barbara , 94

Tomm, Karl, 105, 106, 107, 110

Veatch, Robert, 6, 7, 10, 11, 17, 39

Vine, Ian, 76

Waithe, Mary, 96

Warren, Earl (Chief Justice), 55

Whitaker, Carl, 34, 35

White, Michael, 107

Winnicott, 94

Wollstonecraft, Mary, 54